Real
Writing 2
with answers

ON LINE

Graham Palmer

D1209533

CAMBRIDGE
UNIVERSITY PRESS

CAMBRIDGE UNIVERSITY PRESS
Cambridge, New York, Melbourne, Madrid, Cape Town, Singapore, São Paulo, Delhi

Cambridge University Press
The Edinburgh Building, Cambridge CB2 8RU, UK

www.cambridge.org
Information on this title: www.cambridge.org/9780521701860

First published 2008

Printed in the United Kingdom at the University Press, Cambridge

A catalogue record for this publication is available from the British Library

ISBN-13 978-0-521-70186-0

Contents

Map of the book

Acknowledgements

This book is dedicated to Mary Mantell and her love of Mickey.

The author would like to thank:

Noirin Burke, Martine Walsh, Roslyn Henderson, Caroline Thiriau, Jane Coates and Hazel Meek for their vision, patience and tireless work; and Karen, James and Isobel for hugs and understanding.

The author and publishers are grateful to the following reviewers for their valuable insights and suggestions:

Vanessa Boutefeu, Portugal
Ian Chisholm, UK
Helen Cocking, UK
Stephanie Dimond-Bayir, UK
Philip Dover, Cambodia
Professor Peter Gray, Japan
Jean Greenwood, UK
Sharon Hartle, Italy
Duncan Hindmarch, UK
Rania Khalil Jabr, Egypt
Hanna Kijowska, Poland
Marc Sheffner, Japan
Wayne Trotman, Turkey
Tadeusz Z Wolanski, Poland

The authors and publishers acknowledge the following sources of copyright material and are grateful for the permissions granted. While every effort has been made, it has not always been possible to identify the sources of all the material used, or to trace all copyright holders. If any omissions are brought to our notice, we will be happy to include the appropriate acknowledgements on reprinting.

p. 12: MASTERCARD trademark. © 2007 MasterCard. MasterCard and the MasterCard Brand Mark are registered trademarks of MasterCard International Incorporated; p. 13: VISA logo. The Visa logo and marks are the property of Visa International Service Association. Visa Europe enables thousands of competing member banks to meet the needs of tens of millions of European businesses and more than 300 million European citizens. To find out more, please visit www.visaeurope.com; p. 15: AMERICAN EXPRESS logo Copyright © 2007 American Express Company. All Rights Reserved; p. 18: US Customs and Border Protection 'Visa Waiver' form. © CBP; p. 19: 'UK Landing Card'. Crown Copyright © 2007; p. 20: ATOC Limited for the 'UK Young Person's Railcard Application Form'. Used by permission of ATOC Limited; p. 50: text 'Ladysmith Black Mambazo' from the Wikipedia website http://en.wikipedia.org/wiki/Ladysmith_Black_Mambazo; p. 54: Rogers Coleridge & White for the extract from *Akenfield*. Copyright © Roland Blythe 1969. C/o Rogers Coleridge & White Ltd., 20 Powis Mews, London W11 1JN.

Warner/Chappell Music Limited/Gallo Music International Limited for the original recording *Rain, Rain, Beautiful Rain* performed by the artist Ladysmith Black Mambazo. Written by Joseph Shabalala. Reproduced by permission of Gallo Music International / Warner/Chappell Music Limited. All Rights Reserved.

The publishers are grateful to the following for permission to reproduce copyright photographs and material:

Key: l = left, c = centre, r = right, t = top, b = bottom

Alamy/©Helene Rogers for p. 38 (tl), /©Mike Harrington for p. 56, ©Paul Glendell for p58, /©Mark Boulton for p. 60, /©Mervyn Rees for p64; Corbis Images/©Karl Weatherly for p. 62 (r); Edifice for p22; Getty Images/©Stone for p. 23 (r), /©Iconica for p. 38 (bl), /©LOOK for p. 38 (br); Photolibrary/jtb Photo Communications Inc for p. 23 (l); Punchstock/©Blend Images for p. 10 (l); Rex for p. 50, 62 (l); Royal High School, Edinburgh for p. 70; The Science Museum, London for p. 10 (r) (all); Shutterstock/©Litwin Photography for p. 38 (tr).

Illustrations:

Kathy Baxendale pp. 11, 22, 44, 58, 66l; Paco Cavero pp. 39, 42, 55, 78, 81; Mark Duffin pp. 12t, 13, 15, 30m, 32r, 59, 61, 66r, 74, 75; Stuart Holmes pp. 34, 37, 54, 62; Kamae Design pp. 28, 68; Katie Mac pp. 26, 27l, 30t, 46r; Laura Martinez pp. 14, 18, 19, 46l; Julian Mosedale pp. 12b, 24, 27r, 32l, 45r, 72, 93b; Ian West pp. 28t, 30b, 45l, 51, 73, 77, 93t

Text design and page make-up: Kamae Design, Oxford
Cover design: Kamae Design, Oxford
Cover photo: © Getty
Picture research: Hilary Luckcock

Introduction
To the student

Who is *Real Writing 2* for?

You can use this book if you are a student at pre-intermediate level and you want to improve your English writing. You can use the book alone without a teacher or you can use it in a classroom with the teacher.

How will *Real Writing 2* help me with my writing?

Real Writing 2 contains everyday writing tasks. These include writing email and letters and filling in forms. It is designed to help you with the writing you will need to do when visiting or living in an English-speaking country.

The exercises in each unit help you develop useful skills such as planning, thinking about the reader and checking your work. It is designed to help you with writing you will need to do when communicating in English at home or when visiting another country.

How is *Real Writing 2* organized?

The book has 16 units and is divided into two sections:
- Units 1–8 – social and travel situations
- Units 9–16 – work and study situations

Every unit has:
- *Get ready to write*: to introduce you to the topic of the unit
- *Extra practice*: an extra exercise for more practice
- *Can-do checklist*: to help you think about what you learnt in the unit

Most units also have:
- *Did you know?*: extra information about vocabulary, different cultures or the topic of the unit
- *Focus on*: to help you study useful grammar or vocabulary
- *Learning tip*: to help you improve your learning
- *Class bonus*: an exercise you can do with other students or friends

After each section there is a review unit. The reviews help you practise the skills you learn in each section.

At the back of the book you can find:
- *Appendices*: contain more ideas on how to improve your writing and lists of *Useful language*.
- *Audioscript*: includes everything that you can hear on the audio CD and gives information about the nationalities of the speakers.
- *Answer key*: gives correct answers and possible answers for exercises that have more than one answer. It also gives sample answers for some exercises.

How can I use *Real Writing 2*?

The units at the end of the book are more difficult than the units at the beginning of the book. However, you do not need to do the units in order. It is better to choose the units that are most interesting for you and to do them in the order you prefer.

There are many different ways you can use this book. We suggest you work in this way:
- Identify what areas you want to focus on by using the *Contents* list and/or the *What can I improve?* questions in *Appendix 2*. These questions will direct you to the units that will be most useful to you.
- Go to *Appendix 1: Useful language* and look at the wordlist for the unit you want to do. You can use a dictionary to help you understand the words.
- Use the *Get ready to write* section of each unit to help you understand the context.
- Complete the other sections of the unit. At the end of each section check your answers with your teacher or at the back of the book.
- Try to do the listening exercises without looking at the *Audioscript*. You can read the *Audioscript* after you finish the exercises.
- If your answers are not correct, study the section again to see where you made mistakes.
- When you have completed the *Write* exercise use the *Check* questions to correct your writing. You can also use the *Check your writing* checklist in *Appendix 3*.
- If you want to do more work on this topic, do the *Extra practice* activity.
- At the end of the unit, think about what you learnt and complete the *Can-do checklist*.

Introduction
To the teacher

What is *Cambridge English Skills*?

Real Writing 2 is one of 12 books in the *Cambridge English Skills* series. The series also contains *Real Reading* and *Real Listening & Speaking* books and offers skills training to students from elementary to advanced level. All the books are available in with-answers and without-answers editions.

Level	Book	Author
Elementary CEF: A2 Cambridge ESOL: KET NQF Skills for life: Entry 2	Real Reading 1 with answers	Liz Driscoll
	Real Reading 1 without answers	Liz Driscoll
	Real Writing 1 with answers and audio CD	Graham Palmer
	Real Writing 1 without answers	Graham Palmer
	Real Listening & Speaking 1 with answers and audio CDs (2)	Miles Craven
	Real Listening & Speaking 1 without answers	Miles Craven
Pre-intermediate CEF: B1 Cambridge ESOL: PET NQF Skills for life: Entry 3	Real Reading 2 with answers	Liz Driscoll
	Real Reading 2 without answers	Liz Driscoll
	Real Writing 2 with answers and audio CD	Graham Palmer
	Real Writing 2 without answers	Graham Palmer
	Real Listening & Speaking 2 with answers and audio CDs (2)	Sally Logan & Craig Thaine
	Real Listening & Speaking 2 without answers	Sally Logan & Craig Thaine
Intermediate to upper-intermediate CEF: B2 Cambridge ESOL: FCE NQF Skills for life: Level 1	Real Reading 3 with answers	Liz Driscoll
	Real Reading 3 without answers	Liz Driscoll
	Real Writing 3 with answers and audio CD	Roger Gower
	Real Writing 3 without answers	Roger Gower
	Real Listening & Speaking 3 with answers and audio CDs (2)	Miles Craven
	Real Listening & Speaking 3 without answers	Miles Craven
Advanced CEF: C1 Cambridge ESOL: CAE NQF Skills for life: Level 2	Real Reading 4 with answers	Liz Driscoll
	Real Reading 4 without answers	Liz Driscoll
	Real Writing 4 with answers and audio CD	Simon Haines
	Real Writing 4 without answers	Simon Haines
	Real Listening & Speaking 4 with answers and audio CDs (2)	Miles Craven
	Real Listening & Speaking 4 without answers	Miles Craven

Where are the teacher's notes?

The series is accompanied by a dedicated website containing detailed teaching notes and extension ideas for every unit of every book. Please visit www.cambridge.org/englishskills to access the *Cambridge English Skills* teacher's notes.

What are the main aims of *Real Writing 2*?

- To help students develop writing skills in accordance with the ALTE (Association of Language Testers in Europe) Can-do statements. These statements describe what language users can typically do at different levels and in different contexts. Visit www.alte.org for further information.
- To encourage autonomous learning by focusing on learner training.

What are the key features of *Real Writing 2*?

- It is aimed at pre-intermediate learners of English at level B1 of the Council of Europe's CEFR (Common European Framework of Reference for Languages).
- It contains 16 four-page units, divided into two sections: Social and Travel and Work and Study.
- *Real Writing 2* units contain:
  - *Get ready to write* warm-up exercises to get students thinking about the topic
  - *Focus on* exercises which provide contextualized practice in particular grammar or vocabulary areas
  - *Learning tips* which give students advice on how to improve their writing and their learning
  - *Did you know?* boxes which provide notes on cultural or linguistic differences between English-speaking countries, or factual information on the topic of the unit
  - *Class bonus* communication activities for pairwork and group work so you can adapt the material to suit your class
  - *Extra practice* activities which give students a chance to put into practice the skills learnt and find out more information about the topic for themselves
  - *Can-do checklists* at the end of every unit to encourage students to think about what they have learnt
- There are two review units to practise skills that have been introduced in the units.
- It can be used as self-study material, in class, or as supplementary homework material.
- *Real Writing 2* has an international feel and contains a range of native and non-native English accents.

What is the best way to use *Real Writing 2* in the classroom?

The book is designed so that the units may be used in any order, although the more difficult units naturally appear near the end of the book, in the Work and Study section.

You can consult the unit-by-unit teacher's notes at www. cambridge.org/englishskills for detailed teaching ideas. However, broadly speaking, different parts of the book can be approached in the following ways:

- *Useful language:* You can use the *Useful language* lists in *Appendix 1* to preteach or revise the vocabulary from the unit you are working on.
- *Get ready to write:* It is a good idea to use this section as an introduction to the topic. Students can work on these exercises in pairs or groups. Many of the exercises require students to answer questions about their personal experience. These questions can be used as prompts for discussion. Some exercises contain a problem-solving element that students can work on together. Other exercises aim to clarify key vocabulary in the unit. You can present these vocabulary items directly to students.
- *Learning tips:* You can ask students to read and discuss these in an open class situation. An alternative approach is for you to create a series of discussion questions associated with the *Learning tip*. Students can discuss their ideas in pairs or small groups followed by open-class feedback. The *Learning tip* acts as a reflective learning tool to help promote learner autonomy.
- *Class bonuses*: The material in these activities aims to provide freer practice. You can set these up carefully, then take the role of observer during the activity so that students carry out the task freely.
- *Extra practice*: These activities can be set as homework or out-of-class projects for your students. Alternatively, students can do some activities in pairs during class time.
- *Can-do checklists*: Refer to these at the beginning of a lesson to explain to students what the lesson will cover, and again at the end so that students can evaluate their learning for themselves.
- *Appendices*: You may find it useful to refer your students to the *Check your writing* and *Check your mistakes* sections. Students can use these as general checklists to help them with their writing.

Unit 1
Buy it online

go to Useful language p. 82

- Have you ever bought anything on the Internet? If you have, what types of things have you bought?

- Write three pieces of information that an online store might ask for.
  a _your phone number_
  b _____
  c _____

- Maria Sigala is 25 and enjoys travelling. Choose the best present for her from the online store opposite.

My online store
Perfect birthday gifts

a
Solar battery charger
Recharge your mobile phone anywhere.

b
Electronic sudoku
The fun game with numbers. How clever are you?

c
Walkie talkies
Hold secret conversations with your friends.

Completing an online order form

Look at an example

One of Maria's friends, Aiko, has decided to order her a present from the online store above. This is what she ordered.

1 Look at Screen 1 and find an expression that means *Do you want to pay now?*

....

2 Look at Screen 2 and find an expression that means *Type it again.*

....

Screen 1

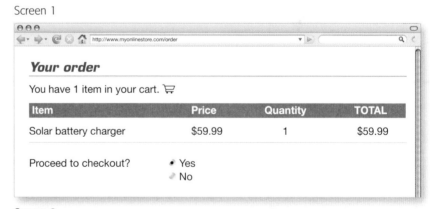

Your order

You have 1 item in your cart.

Item	Price	Quantity	TOTAL
Solar battery charger	$59.99	1	$59.99

Proceed to checkout? • Yes ○ No

Screen 2

Create an account

Email address `aiko@freecell.co.jp`   **New Customers**

Password `********`   Confirm password `********`

3 Look at Screen 3 and find the expressions or words that mean:

a the address where things will be sent

----

b not necessary

----

c the address where your credit card bills are sent

----

4 Why do you think Aiko has chosen to send the solar battery charger by airmail? Circle the best answer.

a She is sending it to a different country.

b The postage does not cost very much.

c It is a present.

5 Where do you type the information below? Write the green number from the billing address.

a your phone number ☐

b your apartment/house number and street ☐

Learning tip

When you come across two similar or confusing words, make them easier to remember by drawing pictures, for example:

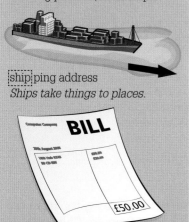

ship ping address
Ships take things to places.

BILL

£50.00

bill ing address
Bills tell you how much money you must pay.

Screen 3

http://www.myonlinestore.com/shipping

Shipping address

| First name | Maria | Last name | Sigala |

Address 1 Via Capella 27

*Address 2 [blank] *Optional

City/Town Verona

Zip/Postcode 37122

Country Italy

Phone 0039045595765

Is this address the same as the billing address? ○ Yes ● No

Shipping options

○ Surface mail
● Airmail

Billing address

¹First name Aiko   Last name Watanabe

²Address 1 7-21-14 Soshigaya

³*Address 2 Setagaya-ku   *Optional

⁴City/Town Tokyo

⁵Zip/Postcode 157-0072

⁶Country Japan

⁷Phone 0081334 837231

Did you know ...?

Addresses are written differently in different parts of the world. For example:

UK/US	Japan	Italy
Person's name	Postcode	Person's name
House number + street	City	Street + house number
City	Area + building number	Postcode
Postcode/zip code	Person's name	City

6 Look at Screen 4 and the credit card below. Where can you find this information on the credit card? Write one letter in each box.

1 type of card ☐ c
2 card number ☐
3 cardholder's name ☐
4 expiry date ☐

Screen 4

Payment method

Type of card:	Card No.	Cardholder's Name
Mastercard	4489012212211248	Aiko Watanabe

Expiration Date 01 2011

7 Look at Screen 4 again and find the abbreviation (short form) for *number*.

----

8 What is different about the Card number in Screen 4 compared with the number on the credit card?

Focus on ...
spelling plurals

Aiko is returning some things to *My online store* because they are not the things she ordered.

Returns and Exchanges form

Date of return: 23 March

Description	Reason for return
Remote control toy car	I didn't order this. I ordered two DVDs.
Blue dress	I ordered two green dresses, not a blue one.

Singular   **Plural**
One DVD → Two DVDs
One dress → Two dresses

1 Make these nouns plural.
  a book   b box   c bike   d toy bus   e watch
  f TV   g computer

2 Underline the nouns in this catalogue description.

> *This diary is ideal for the busy businessman or woman. Now you can buy two diaries for the price of one!*

3 Look: diary → diaries. Make these nouns plural.
  a university   b story   c city   d memory   e baby

Plan

> Maria is very friendly with a family who live in Egypt. They live at 5 El Gezira El Wosta Street, Apartment 6, 1511, Zamalek, Cairo. Their telephone number is 002027372481. The family has a son called Mahmoud Boutaleb who is six years old. He likes football and playing games with his friends.

9 Read the information in the box above and answer these questions.

  a What city does Mahmoud live in? _____
  b What area does he live in? _____
  c What's his postcode? _____

10 Look at the 'Perfect birthday gifts' from the online store on page 10 again. Choose a good present for Maria to buy Mahmoud for his birthday.

Write

11 Complete this online form for Maria. Use information from the exercises you have already done in this unit.

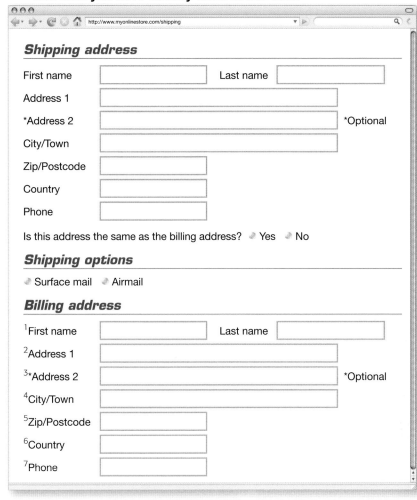

http://www.myonlinestore.com/shipping

Shipping address

First name   [   ]   Last name [   ]

Address 1 [   ]

*Address 2 [   ]   *Optional

City/Town [   ]

Zip/Postcode [   ]

Country [   ]

Phone [   ]

Is this address the same as the billing address?   Yes   No

Shipping options

Surface mail   Airmail

Billing address

[1]First name [   ]   Last name [   ]

[2]Address 1 [   ]

[3]*Address 2 [   ]   *Optional

[4]City/Town [   ]

[5]Zip/Postcode [   ]

[6]Country [   ]

[7]Phone [   ]

12 Use information from Maria's credit card to complete this part of the online form.

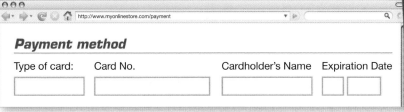

http://www.myonlinestore.com/payment

Payment method

Type of card:	Card No.	Cardholder's Name	Expiration Date

PEOPLE BANK

4978 6783 9624 4250

VALID FROM 06/10   Expiry date: 06/11   **VISA**

MARIA SIGALA

Check

– Have you completed all the necessary boxes?
– Have you chosen a shipping option?
– Have you completed the payment details?
– Have you removed all spaces in the telephone number and credit card number?

E✗tra practice

– Go online and visit an international gift store.
– Search for a birthday present for your teacher or an English-speaking friend.
– Add it to your cart and then go to the checkout.
– As you complete each screen, print it out.
– **Do NOT complete payment details online!** Print out the screen and write in your details. Use Aiko Watanabe's credit card details from page 12.
– Ask your friend or teacher to check the forms you printed out and tell you whether they like the present you chose for them!

Can-do checklist

Tick what you can do.

	Can do	Need more practice
I can complete an online order form correctly.	✓	✓
I can spell plurals correctly.		

Unit 2
Book it online

Get ready to write

- Look at the picture and answer the questions.
  - a Where is Soren?
  - b What is he doing do you think?

- Soren booked his airline tickets on the Internet. Imagine you are booking a flight online. Look at the website below and put the information (a–e) in the correct section.
  - a your name
  - b your credit card number
  - c where you want to go
  - d your phone number
  - e when you want to go

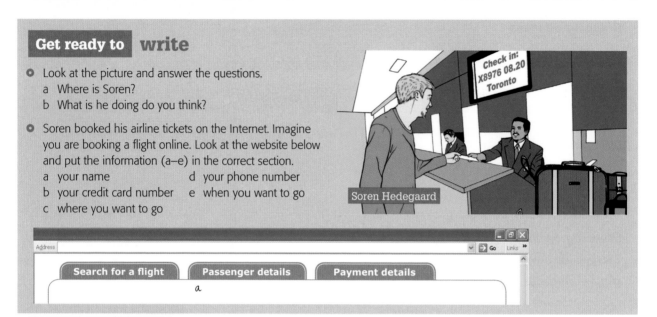

Check in: X8976 08.20 Toronto

Soren Hedegaard

| Address | | | Go | Links » |

| Search for a flight | Passenger details | Payment details |

a

go to Useful language p. 82

Completing online booking forms

Look at an example

1 **Soren is Swedish. He was on holiday in the UK when he booked his flight to Canada. This is the first part of the online form that he completed. Look at Screen 1 and answer these questions.**

a When is Soren going to Canada?

----

b Is Soren planning to return to London?

----

c Is anybody travelling with him?

----

d How do you know which information it is necessary to complete?

----

e Look at the return date. What do DD, MM and YYYY mean?

Screen 1

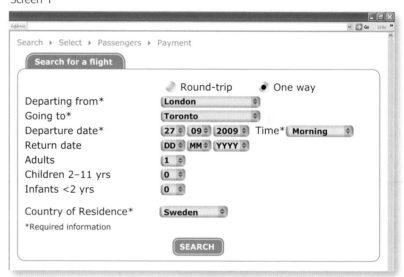

| Address | | Go | Links » |

Search ▸ Select ▸ Passengers ▸ Payment

| Search for a flight |

         ◯ Round-trip   ● One way

Departing from*   **London**
Going to*   **Toronto**
Departure date*   **27** **09** **2009** Time* **Morning**
Return date   **DD** **MM** **YYYY**
Adults   **1**
Children 2–11 yrs   **0**
Infants <2 yrs   **0**

Country of Residence*   **Sweden**
*Required information

SEARCH

Screen 2

| Address | | Go | Links » |

Search ▸ Select ▸ Passengers ▸ Payment

| Search Results |

Flight	From	To	Date	Depart	Arrive	Fare type	Fare	
X8976	London (LHR)	Toronto	Sep 27	08.20	11.30	Economy	$806.67	●
X8996	London (LHR)	Toronto	Sep 27	11.20	14.30	Executive	$1252.67	◯

SELECT

2 Look at Screen 2 and answer the questions.

a What time does flight X8976 arrive in Toronto?

----

b Which flight has Soren chosen?

----

3 Look at Screen 3 and write down where on the form (1–8) you can make a choice from a list.

----

4 Look at Screen 3 again and decide if these statements are true (T) or false (F).

a A pre-flight phone number is the number the airline can phone you on before the flight. ......

b A destination phone number is your home phone number. ......

5 Soren has made some mistakes on the payment part of the online form (Screen 4). Match the error numbers 1–4 to the error explanations a–d below.

Did you know ...?

Some words and expressions are different in British English and American English. Here are some words and expressions in this book that are often different in the UK and the US.

US	UK
zip code	post code
expiration date	expiry date
billing address	invoice address

Screen 3

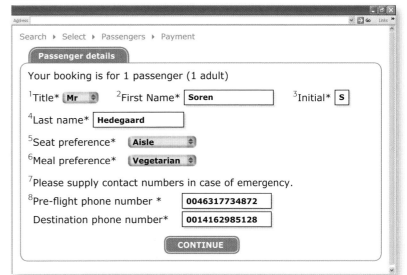

Search ▸ Select ▸ Passengers ▸ Payment

Passenger details

Your booking is for 1 passenger (1 adult)

¹Title* [Mr ◆] ²First Name* [Soren] ³Initial* [S]

⁴Last name* [Hedegaard]

⁵Seat preference* [Aisle ◆]

⁶Meal preference* [Vegetarian ◆]

⁷Please supply contact numbers in case of emergency.

⁸Pre-flight phone number * [0046317734872]

Destination phone number* [0014162985128]

[CONTINUE]

Screen 4

Search ▸ Select ▸ Passengers ▸ Payment

Payment

Card type*	Card number*	Expiry date*
[AmEx]	[4787197217567980]	[06] [2006] ⚠(1)

Title* [Mr]   Initials* [ ] ⚠(2)   Last name* [Hedegaard]

Credit card invoice address

House/apartment number/street * [Utlandagatan 28]

City/town* [Gothenburg]

Postal/zip code * [41280]

Country * [Sweden]

*I have read and accept the fare rules and conditions. ⚠(3) 👆

Receipt

An electronic ticket will be issued. Please provide an email address to which we will send your e-ticket.

Email * [soren175@hotmail.com]

Verify email * [soren17@hotmail.com] ⚠(4)

[PURCHASE]

⚠ **Error!**

a Please read and accept the terms and conditions. [3]

b The expiry date you entered has passed. [ ]

c Your title, initials and last name must be entered. [ ]

d Your email address is invalid or incorrect. [ ]

Plan

6 Soren wants to book a car for his stay in Canada. Tick ✓ the information you think the car-hire website will ask for.

a the date he wants to collect the car ☑
b his credit card number ☐
c his address ☐
d how much he wants to spend on renting the car ☐
e the make of the car he wants to rent ☐
f the colour of the car he wants to rent ☐
g if he has had any driving accidents ☐
h how long he has had a driving licence ☐

7 Write one other piece of information you think the website will ask for.

----

8 Look at the list (a–h) in Exercise 6. Put each piece of information (a–h) under the correct heading on the website.

| Search | Select | Customer details |
a

9 Write one choice that you think the form will ask him to make.

----

10 Below are five words from a car-hire website. Match the words on the left with their definitions on the right.

a economy   1 collect
b standard   2 cheap
c premium   3 return
d pick up   4 expensive
e drop off   5 normal

Write

11 Complete this online car-rental form for Soren (Screens 1, 2 and 3). He does not mind what type of car he has but would prefer a cheap one with satellite navigation. Use information from his flight booking form to help you. He wants to return the car to Toronto airport at midday on 11 October.

Screen 1

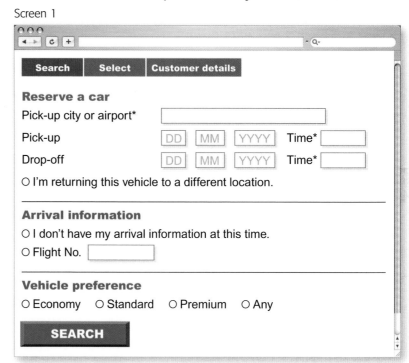

Screen 2

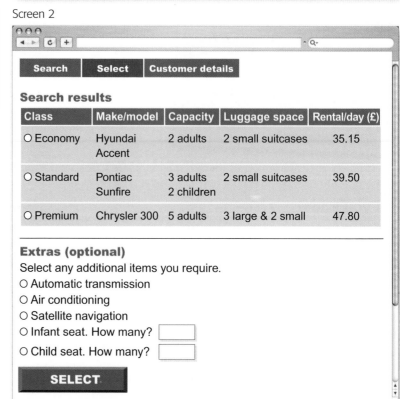

Screen 3

| Search | Select | Customer details |

Customer details

First Name* [ ]   Last name* [ ]

Email* [ ]   Re-type email* [ ]

Credit card type* [ ]   Credit card number* [ ]   Expiry date* [ ][ ][ ]

Home mailing address

House/apartment number/street *
[ ]

City* [ ]

Country* [ ]

Postal/Zip code* [ ]

Phone number* [ ]

○ I have read and accept the rental rules and conditions.

RESERVE

Learning tip

Before completing a booking form, guess what choices it will ask you to make. For example, a booking form for airline tickets will ask you whether you prefer economy or business class.

Check

- Have you completed all the necessary boxes?
- Have you made one choice from each list? For example:
  ○ Economy
  ○ Standard
  ○ Premium
  ⦿ Any
- Have you accepted the rules and conditions?

E✗tra practice

- Think of a time and place you would like to go on holiday.
- Visit an online travel store or an airline website and search for the best or cheapest flight.
- As you complete each screen, print it out. **Do NOT complete payment details!**
- Use the Check questions to check you have completed it correctly.
- Ask your English teacher or an English-speaking friend to check it.

Class bonus

In pairs, help your partner to travel round the world in the shortest time possible! Use the Internet to look up flights. Your partner must leave from the airport in your country that is closest to where you live. They must also stop for at least 15 minutes in three different places before returning to your home airport.
Student A: Your partner must stop in Jakarta, Cape Town and Santiago.
Student B: Your partner must stop in Bangkok, Moscow and São Paolo.
The winner is the student who gets their partner round the world in the fastest time.

Can-do checklist

Tick what you can do.

	Can do	Need more practice
I can complete online booking forms correctly.	✓	✓
I can predict what information a booking form will ask for.		

Unit3
Complete this, please!

Get ready to write

○ Look at the picture of Lukas and answer the questions.
  a Where is he?
  b What is he doing?

○ When do you complete these types of forms? Put them in the correct column.
  a passport application   b visa application
  c landing card   d visa waiver   e discount travel card

Forms that you complete before you travel	Forms that you complete when you are travelling
a	

go to Useful language p. 82

Completing travel forms

Look at an example

1 Look at the visa waiver opposite and decide if these statements are true (T) or false (F).

a Lukas lives in Germany. _T_
b We know his permanent home address. _____
c We know his temporary address. _____
d Lukas completes the form using capital letters. _____

2 Why has Lukas not completed sections 12 and 13? Circle the best answer.

a He has forgotten to complete these sections.
b These sections are optional. He has chosen not to complete them.
c An official will complete these sections.

Plan

3 Look at statements a and b and match them to the correct explanation 1 and 2 below.

a Lukas lives in Germany.
b He is going to stay in Boston for a few weeks.

1 This is *temporary* or for a short period of time.
2 This is *permanent* or for a long period of time.

Arrival record

VISA WAIVER

1. Family Name
| R | E | I | M | E | R | S | | | | | | | | | | |

2. First (Given Name)
| L | U | K | A | S | | | | | | | | |

3. Birth date (*day/mo/yr*)
| 1 | 5 | 0 | 3 | 8 | 6 |

4. Country of Citizenship
| G | E | R | M | A | N | Y | | | | | | |

4. Sex (*male or female*)
| M | A | L | E | | |

6. Passport Number
| 7 | 6 | 5 | 6 | 6 | 0 | 8 | 7 | 1 | | | |

7. Airline and Flight Number
| A | A | 6 | 5 | 9 | 3 | | |

8. Country Where you live
| G | E | R | M | A | N | Y | | | | | |

9. City where you boarded
| B | E | R | L | I | N | | | |

10. Address while in the United States (Number and Street)
| 1 | 1 | 6 | | D | E | E | R | F | I | E | L | D | | S | T | R | E | E | T |

11. City and State
| B | O | S | T | O | N | | M | A | S | S | A | C | H | U | S | E | T | T | S |

Government Use only

12. | **13.**

Arrival record

VISA WAIVER

14. Family Name
| R | E | I | M | E | R | S | | | | | | | | | |

15. First (Given Name)
| L | U | K | A | S | | | | | | | | | |

16. Birth date (*day/mo/yr*)
| 1 | 5 | 0 | 3 | 8 | 6 |

17. Country of Citizenship
| G | E | R | M | A | N | Y | | | | | | | | | |

4 Answer these questions about yourself. Write complete sentences.

a Where do you live?

----

b Where did you stay on your last holiday?

----

5 Look at the landing card and envelope opposite and answer the questions.

a Where does He Ah live? _____

b Where is she going to stay? _____

6 Find this information on the envelope.

a Postcode _110-052_ _____

b Town/City _____

c Country _____

7 Use the words in the box to complete the descriptions of the people below.

school student	~~university student~~
mature student	employed full-time
employed part-time	not in employment

a He Ah

He Ah is studying full-time at York University.
He Ah is a _university student_ _____

b James

James has finished his university course and is looking for a job.
James is _____

c Pia

Pia is eleven years old and enjoys her maths lessons best of all.
Pia is a _____

d Frank

Frank worked as a bus driver for three years and has given up his job to start a college course.
Frank is a _____

e Peter

Peter is a school teacher and works seven hours a day, five days a week.
Peter is _____

f Mary

Mary works for two hours every day at lunchtime looking after the children at her local school.
Mary is _____

LANDING CARD
Immigration Act 1971

Please complete clearly in BLOCK CAPTIALS

Family name KIM

Forenames HE AH   **Sex (M,F)** F

Date of birth | Day | Month | Year | **Place of birth** SEOUL
1 5 | 0 7 | 8 7

Nationality KOREAN   **Occupation** FULL-TIME STUDENT

Address in the United Kingdom 28, AMBROSE STREET, FULFORD,

YORK, YO10 4DR

Signature _He Ah Kim_   EXG 76839

BY AIR MAIL
par avion
Royal Mail

54P

Ms He Ah Kim
104-2 Jeokseon-dong, Jongno-gu,
Seoul, 110-052
REPUBLIC OF KOREA

---

8 He Ah wants to apply for a student railcard to get cheap rail travel in the UK. What information do you think the application form will ask for?

Did you know ...?

In the UK *school* is a place where children study. In the USA *school* can also mean a college or university where adults study.

US	**UK**
semester	term
check a box	tick a box
(on a form)	(on a form)

9 Look at He Ah's contact details and answer the questions.

a What is her term-time phone number? _____

b What is her home phone number? _____

CONTACTS

He Ah Kim
Telephone UK: 01904 448871
Korea: 0082 2 27422354
Email   hkim786@tru.com

Focus on ...

ab**c**def

If..., tick here. ☐

On forms, *If…* sentences usually ask you what you want to happen. Read *If…* sentences very carefully. If you tick the wrong box, you may receive spam, junk mail or marketing phone calls that you do not want.

1 Look at the example below. How will you receive information from the library? _____

> If you would like to receive information about library services, please tell us how you would prefer to receive it.
> Please tick one:
> ☐ Post ☑ Phone ☐ Email

2 Now look at the sentence below. What does it mean? (Circle) the correct answer, a or b.

If you do NOT wish to be contacted in this way by ATOC Ltd, please tick here.
☐

a ATOC will contact you. Tick the box to stop them contacting you.

b ATOC will not contact you. Tick the box to ask them to contact you.

Rule:

a *If… + statement, tick here.* ☐
  Tick here if … + statement ☐
  Meaning: You want it.

b *If + not + statement, tick here.* ☐
  Tick here if + not + statement. ☐
  Meaning: You don't want it.

3 You do not want to receive any more information. Tick ✓ the correct box.

a Tick here if you would like to receive marketing information about new products and services. ☐

b I would prefer not to receive marketing information from you about products and services. ☐

c Check the box if you want to receive further details. ☐

Write

10 Complete the student railcard form for He Ah. Use information from exercises you have already done in this unit. She does not want the company or any other companies to contact her.

UK Young Person's Railcard Application Form

Title Mr ☐ Mrs ☐ Miss ☐ Ms ☐ Other ☐ Date of Birth ☐☐☐☐☐☐☐☐☐☐☐

First Name ☐☐☐☐☐☐☐☐☐☐☐☐☐☐☐☐☐☐☐☐☐☐☐

Surname ☐☐☐☐☐☐☐☐☐☐☐☐☐☐☐☐☐☐☐☐☐☐☐

Home Address ☐☐☐☐☐☐☐☐☐☐☐☐☐☐☐☐☐☐☐☐☐☐☐

Town ☐☐☐☐☐☐☐☐☐☐☐☐☐☐☐☐☐☐☐☐☐☐☐

Postcode ☐☐☐☐☐☐ Telephone ☐☐☐☐☐☐☐☐☐☐☐

Term Address ☐☐☐☐☐☐☐☐☐☐☐☐☐☐☐☐☐☐☐☐☐☐☐

Town ☐☐☐☐☐☐☐☐☐☐☐☐☐☐☐☐☐☐☐☐☐☐☐

Postcode ☐☐☐☐☐☐ Telephone ☐☐☐☐☐☐☐☐☐☐☐

If you would like to receive special offers and information by email, please enter your email address clearly and in block capitals here.

Email Address ☐☐☐☐☐☐☐☐☐☐☐☐☐☐☐☐☐☐☐☐☐☐☐☐☐☐☐☐☐☐☐☐☐

Occupations School/FE student ☐ Part-time student ☐ HE/University student ☐
Mature student ☐ Full-time employed ☐ Part-time employed ☐
Not in employment ☐

Renewals Are you renewing your Young Person's Railcard? Yes ☐ No ☐
If so, what is your existing Railcard Number? ☐☐☐☐☐☐☐
Expiry date of existing Railcard ☐☐☐☐☐☐☐☐
How many Young Person's Railcards have you held in the past? ☐

Declaration

Before signing this declaration, it is important that you have read, understood and agree to the two sets of conditions shown in this leaflet.
I have read, understood and agree to the two sets of conditions shown in this leaflet. I confirm that the details I have provided are correct and I am aged between 16 and 25 years or a mature student.

Signature
Date ☐☐☐☐☐☐☐☐

The train companies may also wish to contact you directly with details of rail offers and other rail-related services.

If you do NOT wish to be contacted in this way by ATOC Ltd, please tick here. ☐

The information collected may also be passed to third party organisations for them to send you offers of goods and services.

If you do NOT wish ATOC Ltd to make your information available to third parties in this way, please tick here. ☐

Check

- Have you completed all the necessary boxes?
- Have you used capitals?
- Have you written He Ah's Korean and British addresses and telephone numbers in the correct place?
- Have you completed any relevant *If … sections?
- Have you ticked He Ah's occupation?
- Have you signed and dated the form?

Learning tip

Because similar things are often put in groups on forms, forms can be good places to find new vocabulary. When you note the new vocabulary, try to group words that usually go together. For example:

employed $\begin{cases} \text{part-time} \\ \text{full-time} \end{cases}$

E**X**tra practice

1 You are going to stay with a friend in the UK. They live at 5, Main Road, Alloa, FK10 2EW. Copy out the UK landing card from Exercise 5 and complete it.
2 When you get to the UK, you decide to apply for a railcard. Copy out the railcard application form from Exercise 10 (or download it from www. youngpersons-railcard.co.uk) and answer all the questions on it.
3 Use the Check questions to check your forms.

Focus on …
spelling /eɪ/

There are three usual ways to spell the /eɪ/ sound.

1 🔊❷ Listen to the pronunciation of this /eɪ/ word and answer the question.
plane   When does your plane leave Berlin?
What is the same about the spelling of these words?
plane   date   state   name?
----

2 🔊❸ Listen to the pronunciation of the words above.

3 Now complete this spelling rule.

Most one syllable words	
We say …	We write …
/eɪ/ + single consonant sound	__ + consonant + __

4 🔊❹ Listen to the pronunciation of this /eɪ/ word.
Spain   My aunt lives in Spain.

5 Complete this spelling rule.

Some one syllable words	
We say …	We write …
/eɪ/ + single consonant sound	__ __ + consonant

6 🔊❺ Listen to the pronunciation of this /eɪ/ word.
stay   How long did you stay in England?
Complete this spelling rule.

Words that end with /eɪ/	
We say …	We write …
/eɪ/	consonant + __ __

7 Complete these words.
   a Somewhere, anywhere. For example: *What … do you want to go to?*
      p l a c e
   b Something you travel on that runs on tracks. For example: *Catch the 10.15 … to London.* t __ __ __ __
   c To give someone money in exchange for something.
      For example: *How do you want to … for your ticket?* p __ __
   d The numbered door you go through to get on a plane.
      For example: *Passengers for flight AA6593, go to departure … 6.*
      g __ __ __

Can-do checklist

Tick what you can do.

	Can do	Need more practice
I can complete travel forms correctly.	✔	✔
I can indicate my preference on forms.		
I can spell /eɪ/ words correctly.		

I'll be arriving on Friday

Get ready to write

- What do you know about Stratford-upon-Avon? Why is it famous? Circle the best answer.
  a William Shakespeare was born there.
  b It has a 'dragon boat' race every year.
  c It has Europe's largest butterfly farm.

- Look at this description from a tour company website. Would you like to stay at the Falstaff Hotel? Why/Why not?

Falstaff Hotel is a small family-run business. It is centrally situated in the heart of Stratford-upon-Avon and is an ideal base for tourists, business travellers and theatre-goers.

Email:
Falstaffhotel@soa.co.uk

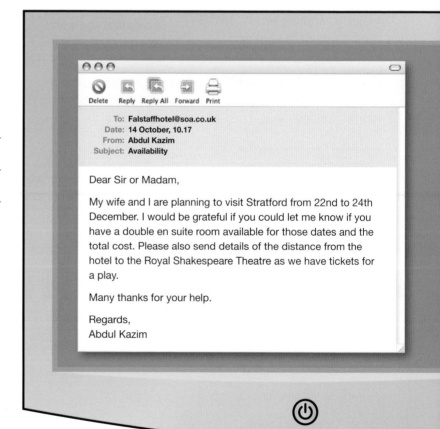

go to Useful language p. 82

A Enquiring about accommodation

Look at an example

1 Abdul Kazim has sent this email to the Falstaff Hotel. Find this information in Abdul's email.

a the people who want something
  <u>Abdul Kazim and his wife</u>
b what they want
  ----
c when they want it
  ----

2 Look at how Abdul organizes his email. Put the things below in the correct order (1–3).
  a Abdul asks for information. ☐
  b Abdul explains why he is sending the email. ☐
  c Abdul asks for more information. ☐

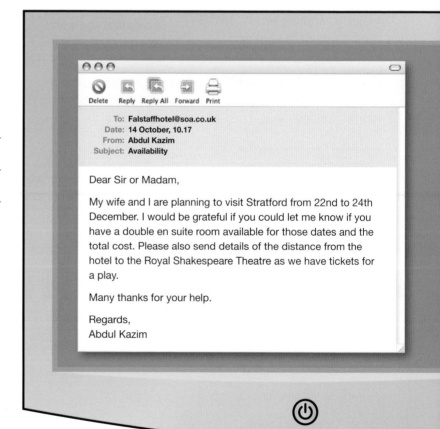

> Delete Reply Reply All Forward Print
>
> To: Falstaffhotel@soa.co.uk
> Date: 14 October, 10.17
> From: Abdul Kazim
> Subject: Availability
>
> Dear Sir or Madam,
>
> My wife and I are planning to visit Stratford from 22nd to 24th December. I would be grateful if you could let me know if you have a double en suite room available for those dates and the total cost. Please also send details of the distance from the hotel to the Royal Shakespeare Theatre as we have tickets for a play.
>
> Many thanks for your help.
>
> Regards,
> Abdul Kazim

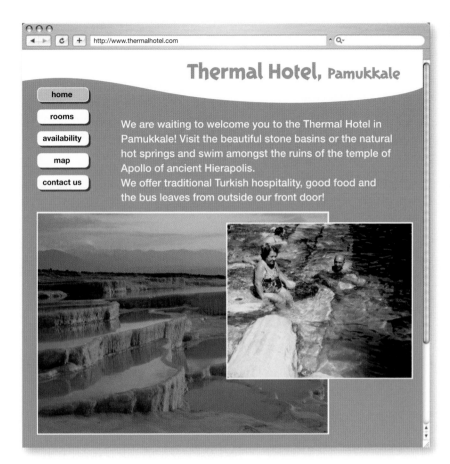

Plan

3 You are travelling round Turkey on your own and want to visit Pamukkale for a weekend. (Circle) the type of room you want to enquire about.

single / double

4 You want to find out about the cost and availability of rooms on 25 April. Write a question you could ask to check if a room is available.

----

5 Write one other question you would like the hotel staff to answer.

Write

6 Write an email to the Thermal Hotel asking about availability.

Check

- Have you given the hotel staff all the information they need?
- Have you asked for extra information about something?

E**X**tra practice

- Think of a place you would like to visit. Decide when you would like to visit it.
- Search for a hotel or hostel on the Internet.
- Write an email to the hotel or hostel to enquire about availability.
- Use the Check questions to check your email.
- Ask your English teacher or an English-speaking friend to check your email.

Class bonus

- In pairs, plan a holiday. You want to go for one week next month. Decide on the dates of your visit.
- Write to a hotel to enquire about accommodation. Your letter should also ask one thing about the place you are going to stay.
- Swap letters with another pair.
- You are now hotel receptionists. Next month is very busy:

First week of the month	Full: no rooms available
Second week	Rooms available
Third week	Full: no rooms available
Fourth week	Rooms available

When you receive the other pair's letter, write a reply. In your letter say whether you have a room available for the dates they want. Also answer any questions they ask in their letter.

- When you receive your reply, read it to see if you can go on holiday!

B Confirming accommodation

Look at an example

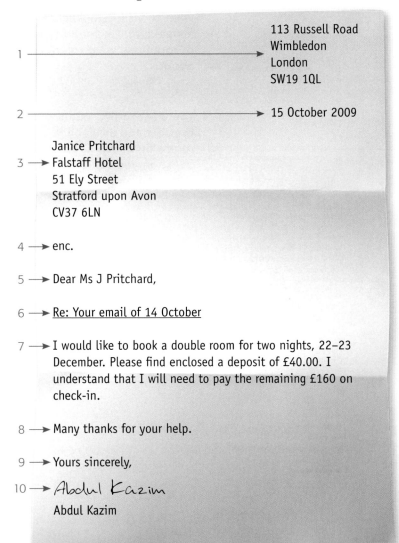

113 Russell Road
Wimbledon
London
SW19 1QL

1 ⟶

2 ⟶ 15 October 2009

Janice Pritchard
3 ⟶ Falstaff Hotel
51 Ely Street
Stratford upon Avon
CV37 6LN

4 ⟶ enc.

5 ⟶ Dear Ms J Pritchard,

6 ⟶ Re: Your email of 14 October

7 ⟶ I would like to book a double room for two nights, 22–23 December. Please find enclosed a deposit of £40.00. I understand that I will need to pay the remaining £160 on check-in.

8 ⟶ Many thanks for your help.

9 ⟶ Yours sincerely,

10 ⟶ *Abdul Kazim*
Abdul Kazim

1 **This is the letter Abdul wrote to the Falstaff Hotel to confirm his reservation. Find these things in the letter and write the correct numbers in the boxes.**

a a shortened word that shows something is enclosed in the letter (i.e. a cheque for £40.00) ☐4☐
b the address where the letter is going ☐
c an expression that ends the letter ☐
d an expression that says *thank you* ☐
e the main message ☐
f the writer's address ☐
g the date ☐
h the writer's signature ☐
i a word that says *hello* ☐
j an expression that refers to another message (e.g. an email or letter) ☐

2 **A letter of confirmation usually contains three pieces of information. Read the letter and put these pieces of information in the correct order (number them 1–3).**

a This is how much money I am going to pay later. ☐
b These are the details of the accommodation I want to book. ☐
c This is how much money I am paying now. ☐

3 **Abdul believes he will have to pay £160 when he arrives. Write the expression he uses to check this.**

I ....

Did you know ...?

En suite is a French phrase. In English it means 'a bathroom that is attached to a bedroom'. Other words that English has borrowed, or "stolen", from the French language include *chauffeur*, *chic*, *petite* and *souvenir*.

Learning tip

When you write an email or letter ask yourself these questions.
– Why am I writing? What do I want the reader to do?
– What information will the reader need so that they can do what I want?
Make sure your letter includes the information your reader needs.

Plan

Thank you for your email. We do have a few rooms available on 25 April. The tariff for a single room is US $30 a night and for a double room it is US $50 a night (or you can pay in Turkish lira). To reserve a room, please send your credit card details and home address. We will charge a 10% deposit to your card in advance.

We look forward to hearing from you.

Bulent Demirci

Thermal Hotel
M. Akif Bulvari, 34, Pamukkale 20280 Denizli, Turkey
Phone/Fax : +90 258 2714564

4 This is part of the reply to your email in Exercise 6 on page 23. <u>Underline</u> what Bulent Demirci says you should do next.

5 You want to reserve a room. Use Ms Watanabe's credit card on page 12 to complete this sentence.

My credit card number is .... and it expires on ....

6 Write a sentence like the one in Exercise 3 to check how much the deposit will be in US dollars for a single room at the Thermal Hotel.

I understand that ....
....

Write

7 Write a letter or email to the Thermal Hotel to confirm your reservation.

Check

– Have you given the hotel all the information they need?
– Have you asked for any extra information you need (e.g. if your room has an en suite bathroom)?
– Have you laid out the letter or email in the correct way?

Focus on ...
as/since and so (linking reasons and results)

REASON	RESULT
a As/Since the hotel has a gym,	you can exercise after a busy day.
b The hotel has a gym,	so you can exercise after a busy day.

Notice the position of **,** (the comma).

Sentence **a** can also be written like this (with no comma).

RESULT	REASON
You can exercise after a busy day	as/since the hotel has a gym.

1 Look at the examples above. Decide if these sentences are correct ✓ or incorrect ✗.
a The play starts at 7.30, so don't be late! ✓
b The play starts at 7.30, as we advise you to arrive early. ☐
c Since the play starts early, you may want to arrive early. ☐

2 Link these sentences with *as, since* or *so.*
a Christmas is our busy season. We would advise you to book early.
   As Christmas is our busy season, we would advise you to book early.
b The play finishes at 11.00. We'll have to eat before we go to the theatre.
c Many people visit Pamukkale. The spring water is meant to be good for your health.
d The food at the Efes restaurant is brilliant! I go there every night to eat.

Can-do checklist

Tick what you can do.

	Can do	Need more practice
I can enquire about accommodation.		
I can confirm accommodation bookings.		
I can use *as, since* and *so* to link reasons and results.		

Unit 5
Don't forget to feed the fish!

go to Useful language p. 83

Get ready to write

1 Home-cooked

2 Takeaway

3 Ready-meal / microwave meal

4 Restaurant

○ Look at the types of meals in the pictures and decide which is, in your opinion …

a   the tastiest?

b   the cheapest?

c   the quickest to get?

d   the most healthy?

○ Someone is staying with you in your home but you are very busy. You have to go out and leave them alone for dinner. What do you do? Circle one answer.

a   Leave them ingredients (e.g. vegetables and meat) and a recipe so that they can cook their own meal.

b   Leave them money so that they can buy a takeaway meal or go to a restaurant.

c   Leave them a ready-meal / microwave meal.

d   Nothing. They can organize their own food!

Instructions

Look at an example

Andreas,

Sorry, had to go out out. Got a football match. I'll be back about 10.00.

There's a ready-meal in the fridge, if you want it. Do it in the microwave:
First press 'Power'.
Next press 'Reheat' and then '5 mins'. (It'll make a beeping noise when it's ready).
Get it out and leave it for a minute before you eat it!
There are also some strawberries. Help yourself!
See you later.

PS - Remember to take the meal out of the cardboard wrapper and to put a hole in the lid before you cook it!

1 Tomas has left this note for a friend who is staying with him. What kind of meal does Tomas suggest for his friend? Choose from the pictures in *Get ready to write*.

2 Why does Tomas not write his name at the end of the message? Circle the best answer.

a   He forgot.

b   He was in a hurry.

c   Andreas will know the message is from Tomas because it has been left in Tomas's house.

3 Put these things in the order (1–4) that they appear in the note.

a   Tomas suggests what his friend can have for a meal. ☐

b   Tomas reminds his friend of an important step when cooking the meal. ☐

c   Tomas gives instructions on how to cook the meal. ☐

d   Tomas explains why he is not there and apologizes. 1

4 Look at the message on page 26 again. How do you write instructions? <u>Underline</u> the correct rule in each pair.

a *Use long sentences / <u>Use short sentences</u>*
b *Use subject pronouns (e.g. You do this) / Don't use subject pronouns (e.g. ~~You~~ do this)*
c *Use the present simple / Use the present continuous*
d *Use sequencers (e.g. First, Next, Finally, etc.) / Don't use sequencers (e.g. ~~First, Next, Finally~~, etc.)*

Focus on ...
sequences

Most sequences are simple and move from step to step. For example:

First / To begin with	*First, put a hole in the lid.*
Next / Then	*Then, cook the meal.*
Last / Finally	*Finally, leave it for one minute.*

Sometimes we want to emphasize an important link between two steps. For example:
Put a hole in the lid before you cook it!

1 Look at the instruction above. Which of these things do you do first? (Circle) a or b.

a Put a hole in the lid.

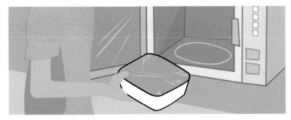

b Cook the meal.

2 Look at these different ways of writing the same thing. Notice the position of the comma (,).

Put a hole in the lid **before you cook it!**
(Do a before b.)
Before you cook it, put a hole in the lid.
(Before b, do a.)
Rule: *before* + second action

After you put a hole in the lid, **cook it.**
(After a, do b.)
Rule: *after* + first action

3 Use the pictures to help you complete these sentences.

First action   Second action

a Before you drive off, check your mirror.

b Before _____

c _____ before _____

d After _____

4 Write three instructions to people who are going to visit your country for a holiday. Use *before* and *after*.

Buy a camera before you come.
_____
_____
_____

Plan

5 Your friend has come to stay with you for a few weeks. You told him you would wash his dirty clothes this evening. However, things have changed and you now have to go out. You are leaving a written message for your friend to explain how he can do his washing. Use the pictures to help you complete these sentences.

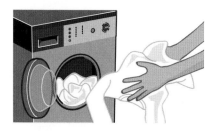

Plastic ball

Washing liquid

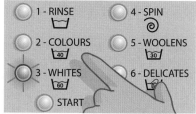

1 - RINSE	4 - SPIN
2 - COLOURS	5 - WOOLENS
3 - WHITES	6 - DELICATES
START	

a First, *put the white washing in the washing machine.*

b Then, _____

c Next, _____

Learning tip

When you are writing instructions, divide the task into small steps.

Use sequencers (e.g. *First, Next, Then,* etc.) for instructions with four or five steps.

For instructions with more steps, use numbered points like in this recipe.

How to make an omelette

1. Put four eggs in a bowl
2. Beat them with a fork until the white mixes with the yolks.
3. Add salt and pepper.
4. Add a little water and whisk.
5. Add cheese and herbs.
6. Heat some oil in a small frying pan.
7. Tip the mixture into the frying pan and fry.
8. Continually fold the edges of the omelette to the centre.
9. Place on a plate when cooked.
10. Serve with a green salad.

6 Look at the picture below and complete this sentence.

Don't forget / Remember to _____

before _____ .

separate whites and colours

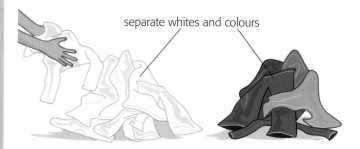

Write

7 Write the complete message to your friend about his washing. Don't forget to apologize and ask him to do it. Use the instructions you wrote in Exercises 5 and 6 to help you.

Check

– Does your message make sense?
– Have you apologized for not doing what you promised?
– Have you explained what you want your friend to do?
– Have you explained how to do it?
– Have you used short sentences?
– Have you written your instructions in the present simple tense?
– Have you avoided subject pronouns (e.g. *you*)?
– Have you used sequencers (e.g. *First, Next*)?
– Have you shown how two important steps are linked by using *before* or *after*?

Focus on ...
linking similar things (*and, also, too / as well, as well as*)

1 Look at some of the ways we can link these similar sentences.

> There's a ready-meal that you can have.
> There are some strawberries that you can have.

- There's a ready-meal and some strawberries (that) you can have.
- There's a ready-meal you can have. There are also some strawberries.
- There's a ready-meal you can have. There are some strawberries, too / as well.
- There are some strawberries as well as a ready-meal that you can have. / As well as a ready-meal, there are some strawberries (that) you can have.

2 Look at where the words in red are in each sentence. Match these words and phrases to their normal position in a sentence.

a and
b also
c too / as well
d as well as

1 In the middle of a sentence, next to a verb
2 At the beginning or in the middle of a sentence
3 In the middle of a sentence
4 At the end of a sentence

3 Link these ideas using the word(s) in brackets.

a My sister likes tortilla chips. I like them. (too)
   My sister likes tortilla chips. I like them, too.

b You can enjoy Thai food in the restaurant. You can enjoy Malaysian food. (as well as) ....

c Fish is an important food in Japan. It is an important food in Norway. (also) ....

d Swiss chocolate is very good. Belgian chocolate is good. (as well)
....

e Mexican food can be spicy. Egyptian food can be spicy. (and)
....

4 Improve the linking in this message.

> Had to go out. Why don't you get a takeaway? The town's got a good Chinese Noodle Bar. There's as well a great kebab shop on the corner of King Street. It sells excellent chips as well kebabs. If you don't like that, there's an Indian too in King Street.

Class bonus

- As a class, write a list of machines that you own that some people might find difficult to use. For example: computer, DVD player, MP3 player, digital camera, etc.
- Each student should choose one of the machines and write a post-it note to leave on the machine. The note must explain how to use it. (Do not mention the type of machine in your notes.)
- Swap your note with another student. Imagine the new note has fallen off the machine it was stuck to. Write the name of the machine you think it came from. Check your answer with the student who wrote it.

E X tra practice

- Make a list of the things that you or your parents do every day in your house. For example: *cook meals.*
- Imagine that you have a friend or relative visiting you for two weeks. You are very busy and need them to do something for you (for example feed a pet or put the dishwasher on). Choose one thing from your list and write the message that you will leave for them.
- Use the Check questions to check you have written your instructions clearly.

Can-do checklist

Tick what you can do.

	Can do	Need more practice
I can write instructions for a housemate, guest or friend.	✓	
I can use sequencers (*First, Then, Next,* etc.).		
I can show how two important steps are linked by using *before* or *after.*	✓	
I can link similar things using *and, also, too / as well* and *as well as.*		

Unit 6
how r u?

go to Useful language p. 83

Get ready to write

- What do you think the man in the picture is doing?

- Do you ever send text messages?

- What do you think is the maximum number of letters and spaces in a text message? Circle the correct answer.
  a 140   b 160   c 180

A SMS / text messages

Look at an example

1 Look at these two messages. Which is the text message a or b?

2 Artash sent the text message to Natasha. What does he invite her to do?

----

3 Are these statements about text messages true (T) or false (F)?

a They use fewer words than emails. __T__
b They use symbols and abbreviations. ......
c They use complete sentences. ......
d They use capital letters. ......

4 Look at how the sentences on the left are shortened in the text messages on the right.

~~Do you~~ want to go out tonight? → want 2 go out 2nite?
Meet ~~me~~ at ~~the~~ cinema at 7.00. → meet at cinema at 7.

Put a cross ✗ next to the types of words that you can sometimes leave out of text messages. Tick ✓ the types of words you need to leave in.

a Nouns (e.g. cinema, tonight) ✓
b Verbs (e.g. meet, go out) ☐
c Pronouns (e.g. I, you, me, it) ☐
d Articles (e.g. the, a) ☐
e Prepositions (e.g. at) ☐

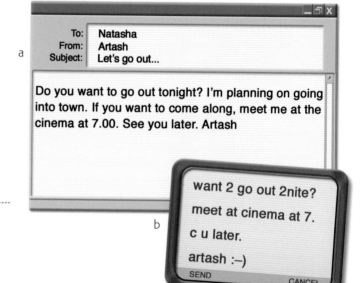

a

To:	Natasha
From:	Artash
Subject:	Let's go out...

Do you want to go out tonight? I'm planning on going into town. If you want to come along, meet me at the cinema at 7.00. See you later. Artash

b

want 2 go out 2nite?
meet at cinema at 7.
c u later.
artash :-)
SEND   CANCEL

Did you know ...?

- The government in China uses text messages to warn millions of people if a typhoon is coming.
- In the past, you had to press your telephone keypad many times to create text. Most mobile phones now have predictive text. This completes words for you automatically by predicting (= guessing) what you want to write. Sometimes it gets it wrong!

Plan

5 Cross out the words that you could leave out of these text messages.

a I didn't see you at ~~the~~ cinema.
b I'm at the North Car Park.
c I've lost my car keys.
d Please can you bring your keys?

6 In English, some words sound like the name of a letter or number. In text messages we often use letters and numbers instead of words. Say the words below aloud. What letter or number can you use to replace each one?

a you = ...u....
b are = ...
c why = ...
d be = ...
e see = ...
f to = ...
g for = ...
h ate = ...

7 In text messages we make some words shorter by spelling them like they sound e.g. *know = no*. Write the standard English spellings of these text words.

a S o m e = sum
b _ _ _ _ = luv
c _ _ _ _ = wot
d _ _ _ _ _ = nite

8 In text messages you can use numbers and letters together. Say these text messages aloud. What do the words in *italics* mean? Complete the sentences in standard English.

a cant see you *b4* 6. = I can't see you b e f o r e 6.00.
b wot about going *l8r*? = What about going _ _ _ _ _?
c wot about *2moro*? = What about _ _ _ _ _ _ _ _?

9 Text messages also use symbols and abbreviations. Match the words on the left with the symbol or abbreviation on the right.

a and   1 cos
b at   2 plz
c kiss   3 thx
d thanks   4 @
e please   5 lol
f lots of love / laugh out loud   6 &
g because   7 X

10 In this text message *cant c u b4 6*, the writer has not used an apostrophe (') in *can't* to save space. Put the apostrophes and capital letters in the correct places in the Standard English sentences.

a Text: didnt c u at cinema. where were u?
  Standard English: I didn't see you at the cinema. Where were you?
b Text: dont no if i can cum
  Standard English: i dont know if i can come.
c Text: she wont b there
  Standard English   she wont be there.

11 Look at Artash's text message on page 30 again. Rewrite it and make it even shorter.

Learning tip

Only use abbreviations and symbols if you are sure the reader will understand them. If you don't know the reader very well, don't use them because they could get confused.

Write

12 Natasha was at work when she got Artash's text message so she decided to email him. Rewrite her email as a text message. Remember to include only the essential information.

> Thanks for the text. I'm sorry that I can't come to the cinema because I'm working tonight. Thank you for asking me. Maybe we could meet tomorrow?
> Natasha

Check

– Does the text message make sense?
– Have you included only the essential information?
– Have you cut all the words that you can?
– Have you used symbols and abbreviations?
– If you have used symbols and abbreviations, are they easy to understand?

Focus on ...
editing for essential information

Before you write anything, ask yourself, *What does the reader need to know?* Your reader will need answers to some of these questions: *What? Where? When? Who? Why? How?*

1 Look at Artash's text message on page 30 again. He asks and answers these questions.
What? A night out. *Where?* Meet at the cinema. *When?* 7.00. *Who?* Artash. (Artash does not give the answers to *Why?* and *How?* because they are not essential.)

2 Look at the picture. What do you think this woman's problem is?

3 🔵⑥ You are going to help the woman send a text that contains only essential information. She has already left a phone message. Listen to the message she left.

4 Read the transcript of her message and underline the answers to the questions (a–e) below.
ANSWERPHONE: Please leave a message after the tone.
SARA: Hi Mark, it's Sara. I need your help. I'm in the town centre and I've lost my car keys. I came in to do some shopping and I had to park at the North Car Park. You know they've had problems here, so I checked the car was locked before I left it. I didn't want it to get stolen! Anyway, shopping took longer than I expected. I've been about three hours. I've just got back to the car and I can't find my keys. I think I must have dropped them somewhere. I've been to so many shops that I don't know where to start looking! Can you please come and bring your keys with you? Call me. I'm not going anywhere!

a Who's got the problem? _____
b What is the problem? _____
c Where is she? _____
d What caused the problem? _____
e How does Sara want Mark to help her? _____

5 Sara has decided to text Mark as well. Four of the questions in Exercise 4 contain essential information that Sara must include in her text message. Which are they?

_____

6 Use the essential information to complete this text message for Sara.

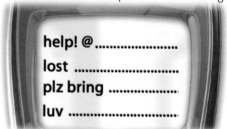

help! @ ....
lost ....
plz bring ....
luv ....

B IM / instant messaging

Look at an example

1 **Look at the instant messaging exchange between Sara and Maria opposite and decide if these statements are true (T) or false (F).**

a IM exchanges are similar to a telephone conversation. You type instead of speak. __T__
b IM exchanges are similar to text messages. You can use abbreviations and symbols. _____
c You can emphasize words in IM by putting them in CAPITAL LETTERS. _____
d People only use essential punctuation in IM. _____
e People only use full sentences in IM. _____

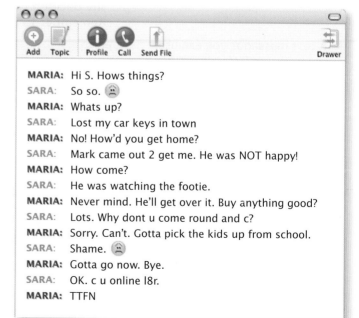

MARIA: Hi S. Hows things?
SARA: So so. ☹
MARIA: Whats up?
SARA: Lost my car keys in town
MARIA: No! How'd you get home?
SARA: Mark came out 2 get me. He was NOT happy!
MARIA: How come?
SARA: He was watching the footie.
MARIA: Never mind. He'll get over it. Buy anything good?
SARA: Lots. Why dont u come round and c?
MARIA: Sorry. Can't. Gotta pick the kids up from school.
SARA: Shame. ☹
MARIA: Gotta go now. Bye.
SARA: OK. c u online l8r.
MARIA: TTFN

2 Look at the exchange again. <u>Underline</u> these things.

a A short way of writing *have got to* (meaning *must*).

b An abbreviation for *Ta ta for now* (meaning *goodbye*).

Plan

3 Match the shortened questions from instant messages a–e with their meanings 1–5.

a You: Hows things?
   Friend: OK/Fine/Good/Not bad.

b You: Wots up?
   Friend: I lost my car keys.

c You: Wot r u up 2?
   Friend: I've been shopping./The usual.

d Friend: I'm stressed.
   You: How come?

e Friend: Saw Johnny Depp in town!
   You: And?

1 What are you doing?

2 How are you?

3 What happened next?

4 What's wrong?

5 Why?

Focus on ...
double consonants

People sometimes make spelling mistakes in instant messages because they are typing quickly and can't spell-check them. Find six double-letter spelling mistakes in this IM exchange and correct them. (The first one has been done for you.)

> **Yoko:** How's your course going?
>
> **Lei:** The Business English part's realy usefull. At the begining General English was easy.
>
> **Yoko:** Is it geting harder now?
>
> **Lei:** Yes. I enjoy the writting lessons but English spelling's imposible!

Class bonus

Work in pairs. Imagine you are taking part in an IM exchange. Do not talk to each other. Use one piece of paper. Student A writes on it and passes it to Student B. Student B writes their reply underneath. Continue until you have finished your exchange.

Write

4 How could you reply to these comments in an IM exchange? Write your responses.

a Wot r u up 2?
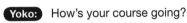 I'm working

b 😩 Failed my driving test (again)
----

c Going 2 have a baby!
----

d Bye 4 now
----

e Got socks 4 my birthday present

Check

– Do your responses make sense?

– If you have used symbols and abbreviations, are they easy to understand?

– Is it possible for the reader to misunderstand your message? If yes, add a clearer explanation.

E X tra practice

– Join an online IM service and use it to chat to your friends in English.

– Emoticons are text symbols that look like faces. They show how the writer is feeling. Find an emoticon online for each word in this list.

a happy

b sad

c angry

d bored

e confused

f cheeky

g rude

Can-do checklist

Tick what you can do.

	Can do	Need more practice
I can write personal SMS (text messages).	✔	✔
I can edit for essential information.	✔	✔
I can write IM (instant messages).	✔	✔

Unit 7
Missing you

Get ready to write

Our Tlusty Czwartek party!

- Look at the picture opposite. What do you think the people in the picture are doing?

- Think of a celebration you have in your country. How would you describe it to a friend from another country?
  - Write the name of the celebration and when it takes place.
    Our celebration is called ....
    It takes place on/at ....
  - What do you do to celebrate? (For example: have a party, make special food, etc.). Write a sentence.
    We ....
    ....

go to Useful language p. 83

A personal letter

Look at an example

> Krakow, Poland
> 21 February
>
> Dear Peter,
>
> It was lovely to get your letter. I'm sorry that I haven't written recently. I've been very busy. Anyway, I thought I'd send you a quick note to catch up with things.
>
> Did I tell you that I started a new job in January? I'm now an assistant in a small boutique in the city centre. It's not very interesting, but the money's quite good and the customers are friendly. My sister's office is nearby and sometimes we meet up for lunch. Do you remember, she's an accountant?
>
> Guess what? Global warming has come to Krakow! It's cold but the snow is melting early. This is my favourite time of the year, coming up to Easter. Last Thursday was Tlusty Czwartek, 'Fat Thursday', and all my family had a party and ate sweets and special biscuits. Mum cooked lots of paczki which are special rose jelly donuts. They were great! Do you have any celebrations like this in England?
>
> Anyway, must go. Hope to hear from you soon.
>
> All the best,
>
> Leszek
>
> P.S. I went to a really good rock concert last weekend ... nobody famous, just a local band called 'Batz'. Have you got any good bands in York?

The writer's news {

Extra news that the writer forgot to put in the letter {

1 Read the letter on page 34 and decide if these statements are true (T) or false (F).

a Leszek has written or talked to Peter before. __T__
b Leszek does not write his complete address because Peter knows it. _____
c Leszek does not write the complete date because it is not important. _____

2 Here are some ways of beginning and ending personal letters. Complete the sentences with phrases from the letter.

a Beginning the letter

Apologizing	or	**Thanking**
– I'm sorry that I haven't written recently. _____		– Thanks for your letter/card/ email.
		– It was lovely to get your _____

b Ending the letter

Asking the person to write to you	or	**Saying you will write**
– I'm looking forward to hearing from you.		– I'll write again soon.
– Hope _____		– I'll be in touch.

Did you know ...?

Emails and informal letters are very similar. The main differences are:
– You do not normally write your postal address or the date in emails.
– In emails, you do not always have to write a greeting (e.g. *Dear Peter,*) or a final phrase (e.g. *All the best,*).

3 In this letter Leszek wants to remind Peter of things he wrote about in other letters. Complete these sentences he uses about his *old* news.

a _____ I started a new job in January?
b _____ she's an accountant?

4 Leszek wants to tell Peter his news. What does he write to show this is *new* news? Complete the sentence.

_____
Global warming has come to Krakow!

Plan

5 Complete these questions in Leszek's letter that ask Peter for information.

a Do you have _____
_____?
b Have you got _____
_____?

6 Do you think these pieces of news make Peter happy or sad?

a Leszek enjoyed his party. Happy
b Leszek can meet his sister for lunch.
c Leszek has got a new job.
d Leszek's job is not very interesting.
e Global warming has come to Krakow.

Focus on ...
apostrophes 1

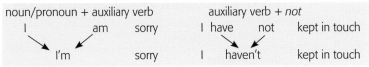

Contractions

I'm sorry that I haven't kept in touch.

An apostrophe (') shows that a word has been shortened and joined to another word to make it similar to spoken English. This makes the writing more friendly and informal.

noun/pronoun + auxiliary verb	auxiliary verb + *not*
I am sorry	I have not kept in touch
I'm sorry	I haven't kept in touch

Be careful!

a it is, it has → it's ✓ it was → it's ✗
b he would, he had → he'd ✓
c **Positive** contractions **cannot** end a sentence or phrase.
  – Will your sisters come tomorrow?
  – Yes, they'll. ✗
  – Yes, they will. ✓

  Negative contractions **can** end a sentence or phrase.
  – Will your sisters come tomorrow?
  – No, they won't. ✓

1 Write the contractions for these expressions.

a I am __I'm__   b will not _____   c she would _____
d we have _____   e they will _____   f were not _____

2 Make these written sentences more like spoken English by using contractions and apostrophes.

a Where is the best place to eat in your town?
  Where's the best place to eat in your town?
b It has been a long time since I heard from you.
c I could not tell you about the party because it was a surprise.
d They will celebrate the Chinese New Year at the end of January this year.
e When you have seen the film, you will understand why I think it is brilliant!
f Here in Turkey, it is the end of Ramazan and we are celebrating Seker bayram at the moment.

7 Peter is writing a reply to Leszek. His letter comments on Leszek's news.

> *It's good to hear that* you enjoyed your party.
> *I'm sorry to hear that* your job isn't very interesting.

Use the underlined expressions to complete these two comments.

a _____
_____ you've got a new job.

b _____
_____ global warming has come to Krakow.

8 Peter wants to answer Leszek's questions about the place where he lives. Match his answers to Leszek's questions in Exercise 5.

1 You wrote about Batz. In York, 'Lowground' are really good. They play a mix of jazz and pop. ☐

2 It's interesting to hear about Fat Thursday. We have a celebration on Shrove Tuesday. It's also called Pancake Day because on that day people eat pancakes. ☐

9 Underline the expressions that Peter uses in Exercise 8 to show that he is replying to Leszek's questions.

10 Complete these sentences about your town or country.

a You wrote about Batz. In _____ (town/country), _____ (name of a popular group) are really good. They play _____ (type of music).

b It's interesting to hear about Fat Thursday. We have a celebration called _____ (name). On that day _____ (what happens).

11 Complete sentences a–c with expressions to show that it is *old* news or *new* news.

Peter's *old* news	Peter's *new* news
He bought a motorbike. His mother doesn't like motorbikes!	His motorbike has broken down and he has bought a new car.

a Do you remember _____ I bought a motorbike last year?

b _____ my mother doesn't like motorbikes?

c _____ My motorbike's broken down and I've bought a new car.

Write

12 Imagine you are Peter and you are writing a reply to Leszek. Use expressions from this unit to complete the sentences in the box.

Thank Leszek
a Thanks for your letter _____ .

Explain why you haven't written (if necessary)
b I'm also sorry _____ .

Comment on Leszek's most important news
c _____
you've got a new job.

Comment on what Leszek has written and answer a question
d It's interesting to hear about _____

_____

e We have a similar celebration called _____

_____

Remind Leszek of some *old* news
f _____
I bought a motorbike last year?

Introduce a piece of *new* news
g _____
It's broken down and I've bought a new car.

Ask Leszek for similar information about himself
h _____
car or a motorbike?

End the letter
i I'll write _____

---

13 Now write Peter's letter.

Check

– Does the letter make sense?
– Have you answered your pen friend's questions?
– Have you used friendly and informal English?
– Have you used appropriate phrases to begin and end the letter?
– Have you used expressions to show that you are reminding people of old news, giving new news or commenting on news?
– Have you used contractions?
– Have you used first names?

Suzie Edwards, Jaz and Dawn live in San Francisco. Suzie works in a supermarket.

E X tra practice

– Imagine that you are Suzie's pen friend. In her last letter she told you that Dawn had won a prize for singing and Jaz had gone to a great museum with his school. She asked about museums in your country. Write your reply.
– Use the Check questions to help you check your letter.
– If you do not have a pen friend already, go to a pen friend website (e.g. www.iecc.org) and get one!

Focus on ...
apostrophes 2

ab C def

Possession

My sister's office is nearby and sometimes we meet up for lunch.

1 Complete this rule.

An _____ shows that something is used by, belongs to, or is related to a person.

Singular noun + 's	Plural noun + '	Irregular plural + 's
My sister's office is nearby.	*My sisters' office is nearby.*	*Girton was a women's college.*
sister + 's = one sister works in this office	sisters + ' = more than one sister works in this office	women + 's = more than one woman went to this college

Be careful!

It's always shows contraction and **does not** show possession.
Look, it's a mouse!   it is = *it's*
I have a pet mouse. Its name is Mickey.   it + possessive s = *its*   (NOT *it's*)

2 Put the apostrophes in the correct places in these sentences.
  a My parents' 30th wedding anniversary is next week.
  b The garage did my cars annual service last week.
  c Suzanne and Giorgi are my best friends names.
  d The childrens auntie is a middle-aged woman with black hair.
  e My husbands family are very intelligent.
  f The towns main street was very dirty and full of litter.

Look at these examples.
My sister's office is nearby and sometimes we meet up for lunch. (NOT *the office of my sister*) *She's not happy because the roof of the office lets in water.* (NOT *the office's roof*)

3 Make these rules true. Cross out the incorrect words.
  a For things and ideas we normally use ~~an apostrophe~~ / of to show possession.
  b For people we normally use *an apostrophe / of* to show possession.

4 Write possessive sentences. Use the words in brackets.
  a My _sister's name_ is Marika. (name/sister)
  b The _____ is *The Amber Spyglass*. (name/book)
  c My _____ doesn't like me. It always tries to bite me! (uncle/dog)
  d My town is in the _____ _____ . (east/country)

Can-do checklist

Tick what you can do.

	Can do	Need more practice
I can write personal letters and email.		
I can write my own news, ask for other people's news and comment on it.		
I can use apostrophes correctly.		

Petra meets Mickey

Jo

Carin

Get ready to write

- Look at the photographs and answer the questions.
  a Jo, Carin and Petra went to two places, Disneyland and a zoo. Which place would you prefer to go to?
  b Which place do you think Jo, Carin and Petra liked best when they visited them?

go to Useful language p. 83

A A personal blog

Look at an example

File Edit View Favorites Tools Help

Address www.blogs.com/jo   Go   Links »

¹ **Jo's Blog**

² **My journal** 📖

³ 21.10 April 11

⁴ **The Mouse and Me**

⁵ Got up early to get to the main park before the crowds came out. As you know, Petra doesn't like scary rides so at first we split up. I had a brilliant time on the Big Thunder Mountain while she and Carin got Mickey's autograph. It's a rollercoaster that crashes out of control into a mine under the lake. Crazy! Everyone was screaming and laughing at the same time. Later we all went on a flight over London with Peter Pan. That was much calmer!

My top tip for when you come to Disneyland: if the queue for Big Thunder Mountain is long, get a Fast Pass from the ticket machine. It gives you time to come back and saves you queuing.

⁶Comments (0)

1 **Jo wrote about her trip to Disneyland in her blog opposite. Where are the things below? Match each item (a–f) to a green number in the blog.**

a the main journal entry ☐5☐
b the name of the person who wrote the entry ☐
c the time and date the entry was written ☐
d the heading ☐
e the number of comments other people have written about the blog entry ☐
f the type of blog it is ☐

2 **Look at this sentence: As you know, Petra doesn't like scary rides. Who does Jo think will read this blog? Choose one answer.**

a people who know her
b anybody

3 In what type of journal would you usually write about these things? Put the subjects (a–g) in the best column in the chart below. (Some may go in more than one column.)

a your thoughts on your boyfriend/girlfriend
b what you did in class or at work today
c your thoughts on a film you saw yesterday
d your thoughts about what the Prime Minister or President of your country did last week
e your thoughts about your sister
f your thoughts about a classmate or colleague
g your memories of childhood

A journal that anybody on the Internet can read	A journal that your family can read	A journal that only your friends can read
		a

Focus on ...
blog headings

Good headings catch the reader's attention.
– They are short.
– They make you ask questions. For example: *Who/What is the mouse? What did the mouse and the writer do?*
– They make you want to read the blog to find the answer to the questions.
– They try to make things funny or interesting. By using words beginning with the same letter, Jo makes her heading more fun. By talking about a person (*Me* in the heading), she makes it more personal.

1 The heading below is in good English but it is a bad heading. It contains too much information. Shorten it so that it only answers these questions: *Who?   What?*

> **Here is some information about my visit with my sisters to see Mickey Mouse in Disneyland Resort, Paris ...**

2 Underline the heading(s) below which sound funnier or more interesting.
Petra's calm ride / Petra flies with Peter Pan / Petra and the Pirate

3 Think about the last time you went somewhere special. Write an interesting, short heading about your visit.

Did you know ...?

The word *blog* is a combination of *web* and *log* and was first used in 1999. A person who posts a blog is called a *blogger*. Adding text to a blog is called *blogging*.

You can set up your blog so that anyone can read it or you can limit its readers to friends and family.

When British people talk about *Joe Bloggs* they are not talking about a real person. They are talking about the ordinary man or woman. For example: *Joe Bloggs isn't interested in how the Internet works. He's just interested in surfing it.*

Plan

4 Think about the visit you wrote about in question 3 of the *Focus on ... blog headings*. You are going to write the rest of the blog. Decide who will be able to read your journal.

a everybody
b friends
c family

5 Think about the last time you went somewhere special. How much information about the place will your readers need? Answer these questions. (Remember: you do not need to tell your readers things they already know but you do not want to confuse your readers by not giving them enough information.)

a Where did you go?

----

b What did you do there?

----

c What did you enjoy about it?

----

d What's your top tip for somebody who wants to visit that place?

Write

6 Use your answers from Exercises 4 and 5 to complete this blog.

Write your name here**'s Blog**

My journal 📖

Write the time and date here

Write the heading here

Use your answers to Exercises 4 and 5 to write about your special trip.

Comments (0)

Check

– Does your entry answer the questions from Exercise 5?
– Have you included information that is interesting for your reader?
– Have you cut out information that is not interesting for your reader?
– Does your headline make the reader want to read more?

E╳tra practice

– Write yesterday's entry for a journal that anybody can read.
– Use the Check questions to check your blog.
– Post your blog on a site like www.livejournal.com.

B Adding comments to a blog

Look at an example

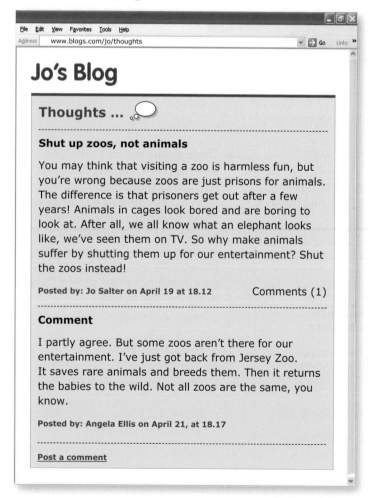

File Edit View Favorites Tools Help

Address www.blogs.com/jo/thoughts   Go Links »

Jo's Blog

Thoughts ...

Shut up zoos, not animals

You may think that visiting a zoo is harmless fun, but you're wrong because zoos are just prisons for animals. The difference is that prisoners get out after a few years! Animals in cages look bored and are boring to look at. After all, we all know what an elephant looks like, we've seen them on TV. So why make animals suffer by shutting them up for our entertainment? Shut the zoos instead!

Posted by: Jo Salter on April 19 at 18.12   Comments (1)

Comment

I partly agree. But some zoos aren't there for our entertainment. I've just got back from Jersey Zoo. It saves rare animals and breeds them. Then it returns the babies to the wild. Not all zoos are the same, you know.

Posted by: Angela Ellis on April 21, at 18.17

Post a comment

1 This is a different type of blog that Jo also writes. This type of blog is very popular. Choose the most important difference between it and Jo's journal on page 38.

a It is about Jo's ideas, not things that happen to her.
b Other people can post comments.
c It's about a zoo, not Disneyland.

2 Who does Jo want to read her blog?

a friends b anybody

3 Read Angela Ellis's comment again. Which of these statements is true? ⟨Circle⟩ one statement.

a Angela agrees with all of Jo's ideas.
b Angela agrees with most of Jo's ideas.
c Angela agrees with some of Jo's ideas.
d Angela does not agree with any of Jo's ideas.

4 Why does Angela write about Jersey Zoo? ⟨Circle⟩ the best explanation.

a It is the only zoo that she has visited.
b In her opinion, it is an example of a good zoo.
c It is the last zoo she visited.

5 Write the expression Angela uses to show whether she agrees or disagrees with Jo.

⟶

Plan

**6 Put these expressions in order. (Complete disagreement (1) →
complete agreement (6)).**

I partly agree. ☐ I don't know. ☐ You're right. ☐ You're wrong. ☐
You're absolutely right. ☐ You're completely wrong. ☑1☐

**7 Here are more of Jo's thoughts. Use the expressions from
Exercise 6 to show how much you agree or disagree.**

1 Poor people are lazy. ....
2 Nuclear power is the best way to stop global warming. ....
3 Testing drugs on animals is OK. ....
4 Politicians always tell lies. ....

8 Match these headings to Jo's thoughts from Exercise 7.

a Earn respect ☑1☐ b It's fair ☐ c Cool it! ☐ d Liars rule! ☐

Write

**9 Choose one of Jo's thoughts from Exercise 7. Write the heading
and the thought in the correct space in this blog.**

Jo's Blog

Thoughts ... 💬

Write the heading here
Write Jo's thought here.

Posted by: Jo Salter on April 19 at 18.14   Comments (1)

Comment
Write how much you agree or disagree. Explain why you agree or
disagree (if possible, give an example to support your comment).

Posted by: Put your name, today's date and time here.

Post a comment

**10 Write a comment to show
how much you agree or
disagree with Jo's thoughts
in Exercise 7 and why.**

Class bonus

Think of something that you feel
strongly about. Write your thought
on the top of a piece of paper
and 'post' it on a display board in
your classroom. Read the other
students' postings and find one
that you agree or disagree with.
Write a comment underneath the
thought. At the end, remove your
original posting and see how much
your classmates agree or disagree
with your comments.

Check

– Remember, anyone can read this. If
you are not happy for someone you
know to read your comment, change
it so that you are happy!
– Have you chosen the best expression to
show how much you agree or disagree?
– Have you explained why you agree
or disagree?
– Have you given an example to
support your comment?

Can-do checklist

Tick what you can do.

	Can do	Need more practice
I can write a personal blog.		
I can add comments to a blog.		
I can write headings.		
I can write for a specific reader.		

Review 1
Units 1–8

Choose one answer for each question.

A Planning your writing

Choosing what to write

1 You are spending a year travelling round the world. You want to keep all your friends and family informed about your travels. What do you do?

  a complete a form b write a note
  c write a personal letter d write a blog

2 You want to tell one friend in another country what you did last week. What do you do?

  a complete a form b write a note
  c write a personal letter d write a blog

3 You want to buy something online. What do you do?

  a complete a form b write a note
  c write a personal letter d write a blog

4 You want to check something about your hotel reservation. What do you do?

  a complete a form b write a note
  c write a personal letter d write a blog

5 You want someone who is staying with you to feed your cat. What do you do?

  a write a personal letter b leave instructions
  c complete a form d write a blog

Knowing the reader

6 You are sending an SMS/text message to someone you do not know very well. Will you use symbols and abbreviations?

  a Yes b No

Choosing information

7 Which of these is the most important information to include in an email or letter confirming hotel accommodation?

  a the dates you want to stay
  b what you are going to do while you stay at the hotel
  c your date of birth
  d where you live

8 Which of these topics would you not include in a blog that anyone can read?

  a my boyfriend/girlfriend b global warming
  c hobbies d fashion

9 What information do you think you would put in the 'billing details' of an online order form?

  a Your address
  b Your credit card company's address
  c The address you want the thing sent to
  d The address of your bank

10 You do not want a company to contact you again. Which box do you tick?

> If you would like to receive information about the company's special offers, tell us how you would like to receive it.
>
> 1 ☐ post   2 ☐ email   3 ☐ phone

  a 1 b 2 c 3 d None of the boxes

B Checking your writing

Checking that the reader has enough information

11 Read this part of an email enquiring about accommodation. What information that the reader needs to know is missing?

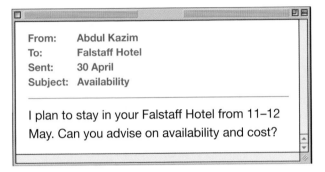

> From: Abdul Kazim
> To: Falstaff Hotel
> Sent: 30 April
> Subject: Availability
>
> I plan to stay in your Falstaff Hotel from 11–12 May. Can you advise on availability and cost?

  a Who? b Where? c What? d When?

12 You have a friend staying at your house. You have written a note to them.

> Meet me in town at 6.00. My bike's in the garage. You can borrow it, if you want.

Your bike is the only one in the garage. It is old and hasn't been used for a long time. What extra information or instruction should you add to the note?

  a It's near the door of the garage.
  b Before you ride it, check the brakes and tyres.
  c It's red and black.
  d Before you ride it, get a coat!

Checking that the information is well organized

13 Pierre is writing to his pen friend. He wants to indicate that he is telling her something new. What phrase could he use?

  a It's good to hear that …
  b I'm sorry to hear that …
  c Did I tell you …?
  d Guess what?

14 Abdul is writing to book a hotel room. In which of these paragraphs is the information best organized?

a
> Re: Your email of 14 October
> I would like to book a double room for two nights, 22–23 December. Please find enclosed a deposit of £40.00 to that end. I understand the remaining £160 will be payable on check-in.

b
> Re: Your email of 14 October
> Please find enclosed a deposit of £40.00. I understand the remaining £160 will be payable on check-in. I would like to book a double room for two nights, 22–23 December.

c
> Re: Your email of 14 October
> I would like to book a double room for two nights, 22–23 December. I understand £160 will be payable on check-in. Please find enclosed a deposit of £40.00.

d
> I would like to book a double room for two nights, 22–23 December. Please find enclosed a deposit of £40.00 to that end. I understand the remaining £160 will be payable on check-in.
> Re: Your email of 14 October

15 Leszek went to a concert by the group Batz last night at the town hall. He is writing a blog. Which is the best blog heading he can use?

  a A great concert
  b What I did last night
  c Batz live!
  d Folk music at its best at the town hall!

Checking layout

16 This is an informal letter to a pen friend. The writer wants to add extra information in a P.S. Where should they add it?

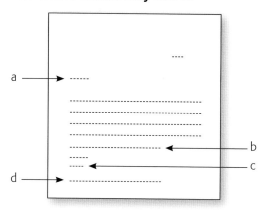

17 This is a letter you are writing to a hotel. Where should you write the hotel's address?

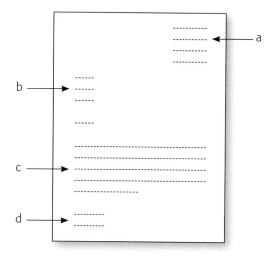

Checking punctuation

18 Look at these two extracts. An apostrophe is missing from each. Where should it be? Choose 1, 2, 3 or 4 for each extract.

a   I¹ve had my horse for five years². It³s⁴ mother was a racehorse.

b   My parent¹s² house is quite small but they like old house³s⁴ and theirs was built in 1895.

19 In this extract, one apostrophe is wrong. Choose the wrong apostrophe.

Whatᵃ's your motherᵇ's name? Itᶜ's not the same as yoursᵈ, is it?

Checking grammar

20 Look at the pictures above. Which of these sentences is correct for this instruction?

a   Before you log off, turn off the computer.
b   Before you turn off the computer, log off.

21 Which of these sentences contains a mistake?

a   Ready-meals are expensive and not very healthy.
b   Ready-meals are expensive as well not very healthy.
c   Ready-meals are expensive. Ready-meals are also not very healthy.

22 Choose the sentence from a hotel website that best describes why guests may want to use the roof-top terrace.

a You may want to take your evening meal on our roof-top terrace as it has spectacular views.

b As you may want to take your evening meal on our roof-top terrace, it has spectacular views.

c You may want to take your evening meal on our roof-top terrace so it has spectacular views.

d Since you may want to take your evening meal on our roof-top terrace, it has spectacular views.

Checking vocabulary

23 Maria looks after her young children and studies two mornings a week. How can she describe herself?

a full-time employed

b part-time employed

c part-time student

d full-time student

24 Noriko wants to text her friend and say thank you for a present. Choose the abbreviation that she could use for *thanks*.

a plz

b lol

c thx

d X

25 Maria wants to write that she is not certain about something. Choose the best expression.

a You're right.

b I don't know.

c I partly disagree.

d I partly agree.

Checking spelling

26 Which of these sentences contain a spelling mistake with a plural?

a My dad was in a fight and had two teeth knocked out.

b At the end of play the score for both football matchs was 0–0.

c All the cities in the world need good transport systems.

d My baby sister doesn't like playing with dolls.

27 Which <u>underlined</u> word is spelt correctly?

a My <u>plain</u> was late leaving the airport.

b My <u>playn</u> was late leaving the airport.

c My <u>plane</u> was late leaving the airport.

d My <u>plan</u> was late leaving the airport.

Unit 9
What can I do?

Get ready to **write**

These are the questions Oleg wants answers to. He has put the most important questions for him first.

> Study Centre
> Opening times? ☐
> Email? 1
> What can I borrow? ☐
> Business English? ☐
> Pronunciation? ☐
> Photocopies? ☐

- Oleg is a businessman. He is just starting his course at Royston College and is in the Study Centre for the first time. Write three things you think Oleg will want to find out.

- 🔘17 The Study Centre manager is going to talk to a group of new students. Do you think she will answer Oleg's questions in the same order as his list? Listen and write the order she answers them (1–6) in the boxes next to Oleg's list.

go to Useful language p. 83

A Taking notes about study arrangements

Look at an example

1 🔘17 Here are the notes that Oleg took while listening to the Study Centre manager's talk. He has made one mistake. Listen again and correct the mistake.

2 Look at Oleg's notes again. He has answered his own questions and added one extra thing. What has he added?

3 Put these activities in the order in which Oleg did them.

a He listened for answers to his questions. ☐
b He put his questions in the order of importance to him. ☐
c He thought of information he needed to know. 1
d He added a note to himself about something else he needed to find out about. ☐

> Study Centre
> Opening times?
> Monday-Friday: lunchtime + after school – 8.00
>   Weekends: 10.00 – 12.00
> Email? In the Computer room.
> What can I borrow? 6 books/1 DVD.
> Business English? Books behind issues desk.
> Can't take them home.
> Pronunciation? Speaking room
> Photocopies? 10p
>
> N.B. Find out about computer room opening
> times.

4 Oleg uses punctuation to make his short notes easier to
understand. Match these punctuation marks with their meanings.

a ? (question mark) ⟍   1 one thing or another thing
b – (dash)   ⟍   2 this is a question
c / (slash or oblique)   3 one time *until* another time
d : (colon)   4 one thing and another thing
e + (plus)   5 one thing (e.g. day) and a *division* of the thing
                                 (e.g. hours)

Plan

5 You are at the same college as Oleg and want to find out about
the computer room. Write four questions in note form that you
would like answers to.

6 Put your questions in order of importance to you.

Write

7 🔊18 Listen to the Study Centre manager showing people round
the computer room and write the answers to your questions. Add a
note of anything new that you need to find out from anybody else.

Check

– Can you understand your notes?
– Have you used punctuation to make them easier to understand?
– Do your notes answer all your questions?
– Have you added anything new that you need to find out?

E X tra practice

– Imagine that you want to use a Study Centre or library. Write notes of
questions that you want answers to.
– Ask an English-speaking friend or your teacher to describe a study centre or
library that they have used.
– Listen to your teacher or friend and complete your notes.
– Check that you understand your notes.
– Ask your teacher or friend to check that the information you have put in your
notes is correct.

Focus on ...
**linking positive and
negative comments (*but,
however, even if, although*)**

Look at the different ways you can
link these positive and negative
comments.
Positive (+)
The Study Centre is useful.
Negative (–)
The computers are a bit slow.

Note the position of the commas (,)
in each example.

The Study Centre is useful but the
computers are a bit slow.
The Study Centre is useful. However,
the computers are a bit slow.
The Study Centre is useful, even
if / although the computers are a
bit slow.
Even if / Although the computers
are a bit slow, the study centre is
useful.

1 Link these comments using the
words in brackets.
a The car is fast. It doesn't look
very exciting. (but)
*The car is fast but it doesn't
look very exciting.*
b This mobile phone sends
video. It's expensive.
(however)
c Your friend is very handsome.
He's not very intelligent.
(although)

2 Find two mistakes in these
comments and correct them.
*The camera is well-made even if
it is ugly. It can take pictures in
the day however, it doesn't have
a flash.*

B Completing feedback forms

Look at an example

1 After four weeks, Oleg finished his course and completed this questionnaire. Look at the form and decide if Oleg was happy with the course at Royston College.

Course Evaluation Form

Name _Oleg Petrov_

Course _English in the Modern World_

Course dates _1–31 August_

Choice of course

Why did you choose to study at Royston College? How important were these things to you when you made your choice? Rank them. (1= most important, 3 = least important)

The college's reputation   ☐ 1
The college's facilities   ☐ 2
The price of the course   ☐ 3

Teaching

How much do you agree with these statements?
Tick one box. (1= completely agree, 5 = completely disagree)

	1	2	3	4	5
The tutorials and lectures were interesting and useful.	☐	✓	☐	☐	☐
The tutors clearly explained to me how I could improve.	☐	☐	✓	☐	☐
I was satisfied with the course.	☐	✓	☐	☐	☐

Facilities

How good do you think these college facilities are?
(1 = excellent, 5 = very poor)

- Study Centre   ☐ 2
- classrooms   ☐ 2
- living accommodation   ☐ 5

Comments

What were your most positive or negative experiences during your studies at Royston College?

> I have really enjoyed studying at Royston College. The tutors and other students are excellent and the lectures are interesting. The Study Centre is also very useful, even if the computers are a bit slow! On the whole, my experience here has been great. However, you must improve the student bedrooms. They're so dirty and the toilets are disgusting!

---

2 Look at Oleg's comments. He makes a general statement about his course (*I have really enjoyed studying at Royston College*) and then explains his thoughts about the different elements of the course. Put these subjects in the order he writes about them (1–3).

a things he didn't like ☐   b things he liked ☐   c why he didn't like things ☐

Learning tip

Before you write anything in a questionnaire, think carefully about how each question wants you to respond.

a Select from a list
Select only one option. For example:
The social programme is good. (Tick one)

Agree	Neutral	Disagree
✓	☐	☐

b Grade things in a list
You can give more than one answer the same grade. For example:
How good do you think these college facilities are?
(1 = excellent, 5 = very poor)
study centre ☐ 2
classrooms ☐ 2

c Rank things in order of importance
You give each option a ranking. You cannot give options the same rank. For example:
How useful were these parts of the course to you? Rank them. (1 = most important, 4 = least important)
homework assignments ☐ 2
tutorials ☐ 1

Plan

3 Think about something you bought recently. What was it?

----

4 How satisfied are you with it? (1 = very satisfied/happy, 5 = not satisfied/happy at all) (Circle) a number.

1   2   3   4   5

5 You are going to complete a Customer Satisfaction Survey about the thing you bought. Which of these questions do you think the survey will ask first? Choose one answer.

a Would you recommend this product to a friend?

b Why did you choose this product?

6 Write a list of positive (+) and negative (–) points about the product.

+

It looks good. ....

....

....

....

–

It isn't made very well. ....

....

....

....

....

Check

– Have you written your name and the name of the product?

– Have you answered all the questions?

– Have you checked that you have ranked (not graded) things in Question 1?

– Have you only chosen one answer for Question 2?

– Have you explained why you would or would not recommend the product?

Write

7 Complete this Customer Satisfaction Survey for yourself.

Customer Satisfaction Survey

Name _____

Product _____

1 Why did you choose this product? How important were these things to you when you made your choice? Rank them. (1= most important, 3 = least important)

The manufacturer's reputation ☐
The product's special features ☐
The price ☐

2 How did you first hear about this product? Tick ✓ one.

Advertisement ☐
Friend's recommendation ☐
Display in a shop ☐
Internet ☐
Other ☐ (Please say what: _____)

3 How much do you agree with these statements? Tick ✓ one box.
(1= completely agree, 5 = completely disagree)

	1	2	3	4	5
I am satisfied with the product.	☐	☐	☐	☐	☐
The product is useful.	☐	☐	☐	☐	☐
The product is well designed.	☐	☐	☐	☐	☐

4 Would you recommend this product to a friend? Why or why not?

Can-do checklist

Tick what you can do.

	Can do	Need more practice
I can listen and take notes about study arrangements.	✓	✓
I can link positive and negative comments.		
I can complete feedback forms.		

Unit 10
Taking notes

Get ready to write

○ Look at the photograph of *Ladysmith Black Mambazo*. What kind of music do you think they play or sing? Circle one answer.
a   classical music
b   traditional South African music
c   rock music

● 9 Listen to this extract and see if you were right.

○ Write three things you would like to find out about the group.

○ Read this entry from an online encyclopedia. Try to find the answers to your questions in the last exercise.

http://en.wikipedia.org/wiki/Ladysmith_Black_Mambazo

Ladysmith Black Mambazo is a choir from South Africa that is noted for singing *isicathamiya* music. They rose to worldwide prominence as a result of singing with Paul Simon on his album, *Graceland*. They were formed by Joseph Shabalala in 1964 and became one of South Africa's most prolific recording artists. The group has now become a mobile academy, teaching people about South Africa and its culture.

Joseph Shabalala formed Ladysmith Black Mambazo because of a series of dreams he had in which he heard certain *isicathamiya* harmonies. *Isicathamiya* is the traditional music of the Zulu people. Following their local success at wedding ceremonies, Shabalala entered the group into *isicathamiya* competitions. They were so good that they were eventually forbidden to enter the competitions but were welcomed to entertain at them. Shabalala named the group after the home town of his family, Ladysmith, the black ox, considered to be the strongest farm animal, and *mambazo*, which means **axe** in the Zulu language, and is symbolic of the choir's ability to "chop down" the competition. They released their first album, *Amabutho*, in 1973. Ladysmith Black Mambazo's collaboration with Paul Simon in 1986 paved the way for international releases, making them widely known across the world.

go to Useful language p. 83

Taking notes from the Internet, books and magazines

Look at an example

1   **Ladysmith Black Mambazo are going to play a concert in your town. Two reporters are working together to write an article about them. They have each read the encyclopedia entry above and made notes.**

Read the notes on the opposite page and circle the correct answer in each sentence.

a   Notes 1 / Notes 2 contain least information.
b   Notes 1 / Notes 2 are best organized.
c   Notes 1 / Notes 2 explain where the information comes from.
d   Notes 1 / Notes 2 contain information that the writer has added.
e   Notes 1 / Notes 2 contain mistakes.

Notes 1

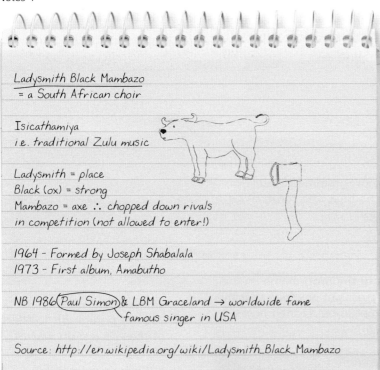

Ladysmith Black Mambazo
= a South African choir

Isicathamiya
i.e. traditional Zulu music

Ladysmith = place
Black (ox) = strong
Mambazo = axe ∴ chopped down rivals
in competition (not allowed to enter!)

1964 - Formed by Joseph Shabalala
1973 - First album, Amabutho

NB 1986 (Paul Simon) & LBM Graceland → worldwide fame
                        ↳ famous singer in USA

Source: http://en.wikipedia.org/wiki/Ladysmith_Black_Mambazo

Notes 2

Ladysmith Black Mambazo

Joseph Shabalala had dreams
and formed a South African
choir in 1965. They sing
Isicathamiya. Name means
'Ladysmith strong axe'. Entered
competitions and won. First
album was called Amabutho.
Met George Michael and
recorded Graceland and became
famous around the world

Plan

2 **Which set of notes do you think will be most useful when the reporters write the article?**

3 **Look at the notes again. Read these statements and decide if they are true (T) or false (F).**

Good notes …
a don't repeat information. ..T..
b put dates in chronological order. ......
c are organized in lists or use diagrams. ......
d use complete sentences. ......
e are linked to ideas/information you already have. ......
f use standard abbreviations and symbols, e.g. *N.B., / etc.* ......
g use their own abbreviations, e.g. *LBM* for *Ladysmith Black Mambazo.* ......
h are organized in the same way as the original article. ......

4 **Which of these sources of information do you think is probably more positive about the band?**

a the band's website   b an encyclopedia

5 **Match these statements about Ladysmith Black Mambazo with where you think the statements come from.**

a They are a national treasure of the new South Africa.   1 a band website
b Until 1975, most of Mambazo's album output concentrated on traditional folk songs.   2 an encyclopedia

6 **Match each online review of *Rain, Rain, Beautiful Rain – The Very Best of Ladysmith Black Mambazo* with the person who wrote it.**

a This is a perfect example of Ladysmith Black Mambazo's *Isicathamiya* singing.   1 someone who bought a CD to see what the band were like
b This is too much of a jumble to enjoy in one go. Cheesy pop covers and hymns ruin what could be a soulful collection.   2 a fan of the band who thinks everything they do is great

Learning tip

When you are selecting a new source of information ask these questions:
– Who wrote it? Why? What is the writer's point of view?
– Are the facts correct? Is it up to date? Does it refer to other sources?

Always make a note of where the information comes from (i.e. the website address or the book's title, author, publisher and date of publication) so that you can look back at your source if you need to check facts. For books, you should also make a note of the page number or chapters you have used.

7 The reporters from Exercise 1 have been asked to write an article about Ladysmith Black Mambazo. How would their notes be different if they were writing an article on African music in general? Circle the best answer.

They would focus on …

a how Ladysmith Black Mambazo were the first internationally successful African group.

b the history of Ladysmith Black Mambazo.

c the life of Joseph Shabalala.

d the life of Paul Simon.

8 🔊 10 Listen to this extract from a radio programme about Ladysmith Black Mambazo and circle the best title for it.

a Ladysmith Black Mambazo's history from 1985 to 1994

b African music

c South African politics

9 The radio station has posted the script of the programme on their website. Read the first paragraph and cross out anything that the newspaper reporters have already written about in their notes.

¹ In 1985 Paul Simon travelled to South Africa in the hope of collaborating with black musicians for his *Graceland* album. Simon asked Ladysmith Black Mambazo to work with him, and they travelled to London to record. The first recording was *Homeless*, composed by Shabalala with English lyrics by Simon. *Graceland* was released in 1986, and although both Joseph Shabalala and Paul Simon were accused of breaking the cultural boycott of South Africa, the album was a success and introduced Ladysmith Black Mambazo into the international arena. This also paved the way for other African acts like Stimela, Mahlathini and the Mahotella Queens to gain popularity with western audiences.

² The release of Nelson Mandela from prison was a historic occasion for South Africa. The apartheid system was abolished in 1991 and the group's first release in the post-apartheid era was 1993's *Liph' Iqiniso*. The album's last track, *Isikifil' Inkululeko (Freedom Has Arrived)*, was a celebration of the end of apartheid.

³ In 1993, at the request of Nelson Mandela, Ladysmith Black Mambazo accompanied the future President of South Africa to the Nobel Peace Prize ceremony in Oslo, Norway. Mambazo sang again at President Mandela's inauguration in May 1994.

10 Look at paragraph 1. Which of these is a short way of saying *the international arena*?

a the world

b England

c South Africa

11 Look at paragraph 2. Underline the expression that means *after apartheid*.

12 How many times will the reporters' notes mention the end of apartheid? Why?

13 Which of these notes is the best summary of the first sentence in paragraph 3?

a
> 1993: LBM + Nelson Mandela collect Nobel Prize.

b
> 1993: Nelson Mandela + LBM collect Nobel Prize.

c
> 1993: Nelson Mandela – Nobel Prize. Takes LBM.

Focus on ...
symbols and abbreviations

Comparing things or ideas

1 Match these symbols with their explanations.

a =   1 more than
b ≠   2 less than
c >   3 not the same as
d <   4 the same as
e ↗   5 decreases
f ↘   6 increases

Linking things and ideas

2 Match these symbols with their explanations.

a →   1 therefore
b & *or* +   2 and
c ∴   3 leads to

Giving examples and explaining

3 Match these symbols with their explanations.

a N.B.   1 in other words
b e.g.   2 this is important
c etc.   3 for example
d i.e.   4 and more similar things

4 Read these statements and use a symbol or abbreviation from Exercises 1–3 to complete the sentences.

a The United Kingdom is made up of England, Wales, Scotland and Northern Ireland.
   UK = England, Wales, Scotland and Northern Ireland

b The population of the UK increased to sixty million people in the 1990s.
   UK's population .... 60m. in 1990s

c The most important point is that we must stop global warming.
   .... Stop global warming

d The price a customer pays is not the same as the cost to the shop.
   Price to customer .... price to shop

e The price to the customer is 100% more than the supermarket pays the factory.
   Price to customer: 100% .... cost

f People want to buy new things. This leads to more things being made in factories.
   People want things .... more things made

Write

14 You want to prepare an article about Ladysmith Black Mambazo from 1985 to 1994. Write notes to summarize the information from the Radio KTN website.

Check

– Do you understand your notes? If not, what would make them easier to understand?
– Have you used symbols and abbreviations to help you summarize the information?
– Are your notes well organized?
– Have you checked that your notes do not repeat the same information in different places?
– Have you written details of your sources?

E✗tra practice

– Think of a music group, sports team or famous person that you would like to visit your town.
– Imagine that they are visiting. Prepare notes about them for a page on your town's website. Use reference books or an online encyclopedia to help you.
– Use the Check questions to check your notes.
– You could give your notes and the website and books you used to an English-speaking friend or your teacher. Ask them to check that your notes are an accurate summary of the encyclopedia entry.

Can-do checklist

Tick what you can do.

	Can do	Need more practice
I can make notes from the Internet, books and magazines.		
I can check new sources of information for opinions and facts.		
I can use symbols and abbreviations to make short, easy-to-understand notes.		

Unit 11
My story

go to Useful language p. 84

Get ready to write

Farm labourer

Soldier

- When do you think both these people lived? Circle one answer.
  a 1799   b 1899   c 1999
- Where do you think they lived? Circle one answer.
  a UK   b USA   c Africa
- If these people met each other, what do you think they would talk about? Write one question each person might ask the other.

  Farm labourer: _____

  Soldier: _____

A personal story

Look at an example

1 Read this story which Les Thompson told when he was 71 years old.

There were ten of us in the family and as my father was a farm labourer … you can just imagine how we lived. I will tell you the first thing which I can remember. It was when I was three – about 1899. We were all sitting round the fire waiting for my soldier brother to come home – he was the eldest boy in my family. He arrived about six in the evening and had managed to ride all the way from Ipswich station in a milk-cart. This young man came in, and it was the first time I had seen him. He wore a red coat and looked very lively. Mother got up and kissed him but Father just sat there and said, 'How are you?' Then we had tea, all of us staring at my brother. It was dark, it was the winter-time. A few days later, he walked away and my mother stood right out in the middle of the road, watching. He was going to fight in South Africa. He walked smartly down the lane until his red coat was no bigger than a poppy. Then the tree hid him. We never saw him again.

2 How do you think Len felt when he was waiting for his brother to come home? Circle the best answer.

   a excited
   b confused
   c lonely

3 Why did his brother leave again? Circle the best answer.

   a Because he had to go to war.
   b Because he didn't like his father.
   c Because he did not have a job.

4 How do you think Len felt after his brother left? Circle the best answer.

   a excited
   b confused
   c lonely

5 **Why do you think this event was important to three-year-old Len?** Circle **the best answer.**

a   It was exciting to meet his brother.
b   Len knew he wouldn't see his brother again.
c   He liked soldiers.

6 **Why do you think the event was important to 71-year-old Len?** Circle **the best answer.**

a   It was the first and last time he saw his brother.
b   He enjoys thinking about his childhood.
c   He likes to think his brother was important because he travelled.

Did you know …?

Len's story is an example of a *flashbulb memory*. These strong memories are like photographs that capture a moment in time. They are normally linked to an event that made you very happy, sad or upset. Because they are important to you, you think about them a lot and sometimes tell other people about them. The memory can change slightly each time you think or talk about it. Writing a memory down 'fixes' it and makes it unlikely to change.

---

7 **Match the phrases on the left with the headings on the right.**

a   There were ten of us in the family …   1   The event
b   He arrived about six in the evening …   2   What happened after the event
c   A few days later he walked away …   3   Background to the event

8 **Write these questions in the correct places in the notes.**

What happened?   Who?   Where?

a ....
A small child, mother, father and much older brother.

b ....
A farm in England in 1899.

c ....
The brother returned home after a long time and then left again. He didn't return.

9 **Look at the way Len chose to describe the soldier's arrival.**

Mother got up and kissed him but *Father* just *sat there and said, 'How are you?'*

Why does Len emphasize that his father chose not to stand up? Circle **the best answer.**

a   It shows that Len thinks his father was wrong.
b   It shows that Len's father was ill.

10 **How do you think Len's father would feel, if he read the story?** Circle **the best answer.**

a   happy
b   unhappy

11 **Rewrite the sentence from Exercise 9 so that it would not upset Len's father. (Tip: use *and*)**

....
....
....

Learning tip

Some verbs in English are regular. You add *–ed* to make the past simple. For example:
walk → walked
Irregular verbs do not make the past simple in this way. For example:
do → did, go → went, get → got, eat → ate

Try learning the past simple forms of six irregular verbs at a time. To help you, write a sentence for each one and draw a picture. For example:
I *came* to Paris yesterday.

Later, look at the picture and try to remember the sentence.

---

12 **Write the irregular past simple form of these verbs from Len's story.**

a   come ......*came*......
b   wear ....
c   sit ....
d   have ....
e   stand ....
f   hide ....
g   see ....

Did you know …?

In the First World War, John McCrae, a Canadian doctor, wrote a poem called *In Flanders' Fields*. It focused on the fact that poppies were the only plant that grew on the battlefields. Since then the poppy has become a symbol in the UK. Many people wear red paper poppies on 11 November (Remembrance Day) to show that they remember soldiers who have died in battle.

13 Look at the *Did you know …?* box above. In the story Len says:

He walked smartly down the lane until his red coat was no bigger than a poppy.

What do you think the British reader will understand? Circle the best answer.

a Len's brother probably died. That is why he chooses a poppy to describe the red coat.

b Len likes flowers. That is why he describes his brother as a poppy.

c Children like bright colours. The coat was the colour of a poppy and easy to remember.

Plan

14 Your local magazine prints a story every week about a childhood experience from one of its readers. Plan a short story for the magazine about the most important event that happened to you when you were a child. Answer these questions.

a What was the event?

b How did you feel before the event?

c What caused the event?

d What did you feel like afterwards?

e Why was the event important to you?

Focus on …
symbolism

A symbol is a sign. It represents something else. When a writer uses a symbol in a story it can help the reader to understand what they are trying to say. Different cultures use different symbols. Here are some popular symbols in English stories.

Someone inside, looking out of a window *represents* feeling trapped.
Someone outside in natural surroundings *represents* freedom from rules.
Animals and plants *represent* wild nature.
Machines and buildings *represent* how humans change nature.

1 What might these things represent? Match the symbol to a possible meaning.

a a key — 1 anger
b a locked door 2 lack of choice
c a fist 3 education
d an open hand 4 friendliness
e a book — 5 choice or opportunity

2 What do you think these symbols in the story represent?
a the red coat *the army / loss (of people)*
b the tree _____
c the mother standing in the middle of the road
_____

15 Complete this chart to help you think about your story.

Who? (A maximum of three people. What are they like?)	
Where? (A maximum of two places)	
What happened?	

16 Write two sentences to explain the background to the event. Use the past simple and be careful with the past tense of irregular verbs.

_____
_____
_____
_____
_____

Focus on ...
time sequencers

We often use time sequencers to show that one thing happened after another. For example:
He walked smartly down the lane … Then the tree hid him.

Look at these examples of time sequencers. Notice the commas (,).
He came to stay. A few days later, /Later, he went away again.
He came to stay. After that, / Afterwards, / After a few days, he went away again.
After he came to stay, he went away again.

Rule:
After is not used on its own.
✗ *He came to stay. After, he went away again.* ✗

1 Look at the time sequencers in these sentences. Are they correct (✓) or incorrect (✗)?
   a US President Kennedy was shot in 1980. Later, his killer was also shot. ✓
   b The Chinese invented fireworks. After, the Germans made rockets that could reach space. ☐
   c Tchaikovsky wrote *Sleeping Beauty* in 1890. Three years later, he died. ☐
   d Imelda Marcos left the Philippines. Afterwards she said, 'I did not have 3,000 pairs of shoes. I had 1,060.' ☐

2 Rewrite any incorrect sentence(s).

Write

17 Write your story. Remember that friends, family and strangers will buy the magazine. While you are writing it, ask yourself: is there anything I want to leave out because it will upset some of my readers, friends or family?

18 Read your story and think about how you can give it extra meaning. Think of a symbol that will help the reader understand the meaning of your story.

19 Rewrite your story to include the symbol.

Check

– Does the story make sense?
– Have you only included things that you are happy for your readers to know?
– Do the readers understand how you felt before the event and afterwards?
– Do the readers understand the background to the event?
– Have you used some sequencers to help the reader understand when things happened?
– Have you used one or two symbols in your story?

E✗tra practice

– Write a story of about 200 words for the local magazine about ONE of these things.
   a The most important / thing that you did wrong / thing you lost, forgot or broke / disagreement or fight you have had / thing you have achieved
   b An emergency
   c A time when something happened that you were not prepared for
   d A time when someone found you doing something wrong (e.g. telling a lie, committing a crime, etc.)
   e A time you heard a secret or went to a forbidden place
   f A time that something bad happened to you which had unexpected good results
– Use the Check questions to check your story.

Can-do checklist

Tick what you can do.

	Can do	Need more practice
I can write a personal story.		
I can add symbolism to give a story extra meaning.		
I can use time sequencers (*Later/Then/Afterwards*, etc.) to show when things happened in a story.		

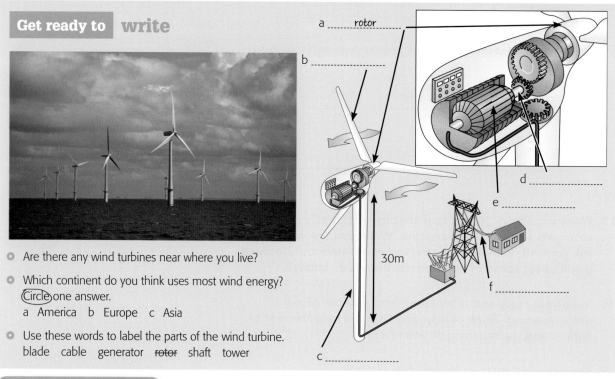

a .... rotor ....

b ....

d ....

e ....

30m

f ....

c ....

- Are there any wind turbines near where you live?
- Which continent do you think uses most wind energy? Circle one answer.
  a America b Europe c Asia
- Use these words to label the parts of the wind turbine.
  blade cable generator ~~rotor~~ shaft tower

go to Useful language p. 84

Describing a process

Look at an example

1 You work for a company that makes environmentally-friendly products. This is part of a page from the company's website. Read it and find out if you labelled the diagram correctly in *Get ready to write*.

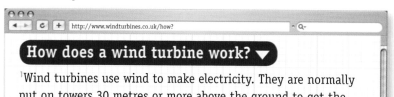

http://www.windturbines.co.uk/how?

How does a wind turbine work? ▼

[1]Wind turbines use wind to make electricity. They are normally put on towers 30 metres or more above the ground to get the most energy from faster winds. [2]The energy in the wind turns three blades around a rotor at 10–30 revolutions per minute. Inside the turbine, the rotor spins a shaft which is connected to a generator. This generates electricity. [3]Wind turbines can be used to produce electricity for a single home or building or they can be connected to an electricity grid. Electricity is then sent through cables to homes, businesses, schools and so on.

Did you know ...?

- Wind has been used to power ships for thousands of years.
- The Chinese first used wind-power to pump water over 4,000 years ago.
- Wind is now the fastest growing energy source worldwide.
- There are wind turbines in the Arctic.
- Modern wind turbines can work for over 20 years without stopping once.

2 Match these explanations to information from the webpage. Write the blue number from the webpage.

a What happens to the electricity ☐3

b How wind turbines make electricity ☐

c What a wind turbine is ☐

3 Decide if these statements are true (T) or false (F).

a The writer explains why they like wind turbines. ..F..

b The writer explains why they dislike wind turbines. ....

c The writer explains the facts about how wind turbines work. ....

d The company has designed the web-page for experts in wind-power. ....

e The company has designed the web-page for people who do not know very much about wind-power. ....

4 Look at the language in this description from a personal website. It is very different from the language used in the business website on page 58.

> Wind turbines are cool! They're normally put on great big towers but I've got one on my house. I use it to power my TV. Only problem, when the wind stops ... no TV!

Decide if these rules are true for business/scientific descriptions or personal descriptions. Put each rule (a–f) in the correct box below.

a Use neutral language

b Use slang, e.g. *cool*

c Use contractions, e.g. *They're*

d Do not use contractions

e Use complete sentences

f Shorten sentences (for example: ~~The~~ Only problem ~~is that~~ when the wind stops ~~there is~~ no TV.)

Business/scientific descriptions	Personal descriptions
a	

Focus on ...
the passive form

Wind turbines *make* electricity.　(The writer focuses on
　　　　　↑　　　　　　　　　　**what** wind turbines **do**.)
　　Subject

Are you interested in **what the subject does**?
Yes → Use an active verb form

The turbine *is connected* to a generator.　(The writer focuses on **how**
　　↑　　　　　　　　　　　　　　the turbine **works**.)
　Subject

Are you more interested in **what happens to the subject**?
Yes → Use a passive verb form (*am/are/is* + past participle)

The turbine is connected to a generator　(The writer focuses on **how** the
by a shaft.　　　　　　　　　　　　turbine and generator **are connected**.)

Is it important to understand **what/who makes something happen** to the subject?
Yes → Use a passive verb form + *by* ....

1 Look at the pairs of sentences below. Circle the sentences which are written in the passive form.

a ①　Wind turbines are normally mounted on towers.

　2　Electricity companies normally mount wind turbines on towers.

b 1　The wind turns three blades.

　2　Three blades are turned by the wind.

c 1　People can use them to generate electricity for a single home.

　2　They can be used to produce electricity for a single home.

2 Put the verb in the active or passive form in these sentences. Use the verb in brackets.

a Wind turbines can _be connected_ to the national grid by electricity companies. (*connect*)

b Radios _____ electricity. (*use*)

c Batteries _____ electricity. (*store*)

d Some batteries can _____ at home. (*recharge*)

e You can _____ some old clocks with a key. (*wind up*)

Plan

5 When do you think it might be useful to have a wind up radio? (Circle) the best answers.

a when you go camping
b when you go diving
c when you travel or live in a remote area
d when there is an emergency situation and you have no electricity

6 (Circle) the handle in the picture on the right.

7 What do you think the handle does? (Circle) the best answer.

a recharges the battery
b turns the radio on
c makes music

8 Write two questions about wind-up radios that you would like to know the answers to.

----

9 A colleague has written these notes on wind-up radios. Try to find the answers to the questions you wrote in Exercise 8.

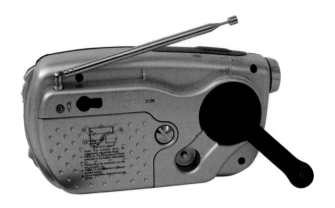

What a wind-up radio is
- uses hand-power to generate electricity
- developed to help people in places where there isn't an electricity grid
- some wind-up radios are also torches

How it works
- turn the handle to wind it up
- handle connects to a small generator
- turning the handle turns the generator, makes electricity
- battery stores electricity
- to recharge battery wind for 30 seconds = 30 minutes music

Did you know ...?

– The wind-up radio was invented by Trevor Baylis in 1993 and developed by a company in South Africa.
– A $100 wind-up laptop computer was invented by Nicholas Negroponte from MIT in 2005. It is designed to help children's education in the developing world.

Learning tip

Wind has two different meanings and two different pronunciations, /wɪnd/ and /waɪnd/.

1 🔊 11 Listen to the pronunciation of *wind* in these sentences.
   a Wind turbines use wind to make electricity. /wɪnd/
   b 35,000 wind-up radios were given to the people of Aceh after a tsunami in 2005. /waɪnd/

2 Decide how you pronounce the word *wind* in these sentences: 1 /wɪnd/ or 2 /waɪnd/. Write 1 or 2 in the boxes.
   a Your watch has stopped. You need to wind it up. [2]
   b Can you hear the wind in the trees? [ ]
   c I was cold in the back of the car, so I asked the driver to wind his window up. [ ]
   d A hurricane is a very fast wind. [ ]

3 🔊 12 Listen and check your answers.

Focus on ...
linking ideas and thoughts

In sentences, we use *and*, *or* and *but* to show how our ideas and thoughts are linked. In complete pieces of writing, we show how ideas and thoughts are linked in different ways. Here are three of the most common ways.

1 General → Specific → More specific
   What a wind turbine is
   → How wind turbines make electricity
   → What happens to the electricity

2 Noun → Pronoun
   Wind turbines use wind to make electricity. They are normally put on towers 30 metres or more above the ground to get the most energy from faster winds.

3 Full name → Abbreviation
   The Massachusetts Institute of Technology (MIT) is one of America's leading colleges. MIT is a world leader in many areas of technological research.

Look at these sentences from a webpage about a different kind of process. They are about how students can apply to study at a university in the UK. Put the sentences in the best order (1–4) to make a complete text. Use the linking patterns above to help you. Each word in green links to an idea in pink in another sentence.

Applying to a University in the UK

a Applications have to be made before mid-January. ☐

b There are 329 different universities and colleges in the UK. 1

c For most full-time courses you can apply online through the UCAS website. ☐

d Applications to study at them are organized by the University and Colleges Admissions Service (UCAS). ☐

Write

10 **You have been asked to add a page to your company's website. Use the notes from Exercise 9 to write a description of how wind-up radios work.**

Check

– Does your description make sense?
– Does it follow the patterns for linking ideas and thoughts?
– Have you used active verb forms where the reader is interested in what something does?
– Have you used passive verb forms where the reader is interested in what happens to something?

E X tra practice

a   b   c

1 Choose one of these subjects.
   a How solar-powered torches work
   b How tumble dryers work
   c How to get a driving licence in your country
2 Write one fact you already know about the subject.

Write two questions about the subject that you would like to find the answers to.

----

4 Look up the answers in books or on the Internet.
5 Write a description of the process for a company or government website.
6 Use the Check questions to check your description of the process.
7 Ask a teacher or an English-speaking friend to check that your description is logical and clear.

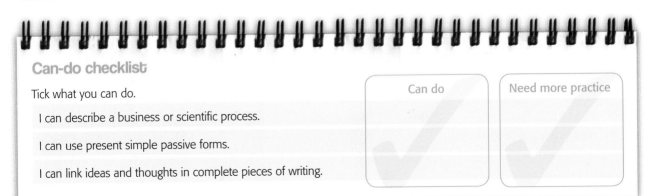

Can-do checklist

Tick what you can do.

	Can do	Need more practice
I can describe a business or scientific process.	✓	✓
I can use present simple passive forms.		
I can link ideas and thoughts in complete pieces of writing.		

Unit 13
I'm going to talk about ...

Get ready to write

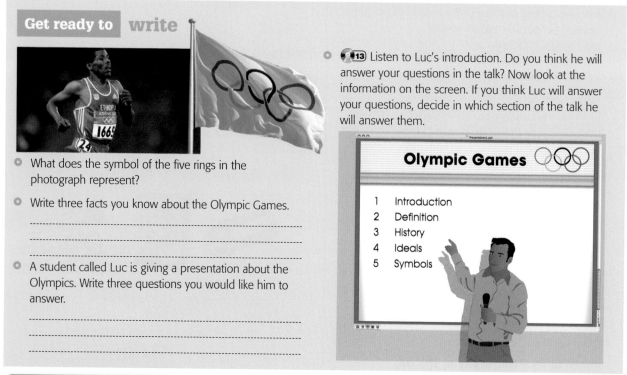

- What does the symbol of the five rings in the photograph represent?

- Write three facts you know about the Olympic Games.

- A student called Luc is giving a presentation about the Olympics. Write three questions you would like him to answer.

○ 🔊 13 Listen to Luc's introduction. Do you think he will answer your questions in the talk? Now look at the information on the screen. If you think Luc will answer your questions, decide in which section of the talk he will answer them.

Olympic Games ◯◯◯

1 Introduction
2 Definition
3 History
4 Ideals
5 Symbols

go to Useful language p. 84

A Notes for a presentation

Look at an example

Here are the cue cards with the notes that Luc used to help him remember the introduction and the first part of his talk.

1

INTRODUCTION   (Slide 1)
- Greet people   1 Introduce myself.
- The Olympics?   X Just overpaid sports people? X
- 4 sections: 1 definition
                    2 history
                    3 Ideals
                    4 symbols
— Questions: end of each section.

2

DEFINITION   (Slide 2)
International multi-sport event
- International: first games — 14 countries
                   now — 200+ (more than recognized by the UN)
- Multi-sport event: first — 8 sports
                   (athletics, cycling, fencing, gymnastics, weightlifting,
                   shooting, swimming, wrestling)
                   2012 — 26 sports
                   Winter Games: skiing, figure-skating, ice-hockey, etc.
- Event: Summer Games — every 4 years
                   WG + SG — 2 years apart
- Questions?

1 Decide if these statements about the cue cards are true (T) or false (F).

They …

a will not be given to the audience ..T..
b are a summary of the essential points ......
c include everything that you are going to say ......
d help you remember the structure of the talk ......
e are written in complete sentences ......
f help you remember essential facts ......
g include cues that remind you to do things ......
h include notes about the visual aid (e.g. slide) you are going to use ......

2 Why do you think Luc has highlighted some words in yellow on cue card 2? (Circle) the best answer.

a they are essential facts to make his point
b they are numbers
c they are extra information

Plan

3 You are going to help Luc write a cue card for a section of his presentation. This section divides logically into two parts. Put a slash (/) where the section should be divided.

> Months before a modern Games starts, the Olympic flame is lit from the sun's rays at Olympia, the home of the ancient Olympics. It is then carried by athletes in a relay to the venue for the Games and burns all the time the competitions are taking place. It symbolizes the link between the ancient and modern Games and the handing down of knowledge, life and spirit from generation to generation. The flag is a symbol of international friendship. The five linked rings on it represent the five continents linked together. Each ring is a different colour so that the flag contains colours that are used in all the national flags of the world.

4 Write this sentence in note form.

The two main symbols of the Olympic Games are the Olympic flame and the flag.

----

5 Write a heading for the first section of the text from Exercise 3 in no more than one word.

6 Complete these notes.

- lit from ___sun's rays___ at _____ →
  (relay) → modern venue
- burns during games
- links _____ → _____
- symbolizes knowledge, _____ and _____

7 Write a heading for the second section of the text from Exercise 3 in no more than one word.

----

8 Complete these notes.

- symbolizes _____
- 5 rings = _____
- 5 colours - _____

9 Write this summary in note form.

> So the flame and the flag represent what the Olympics is all about: friendship between countries.

Write

10 Use Exercises 3–9 to help Luc write notes for the Symbols section of his presentation. Do not forget to highlight the most important information.

SYMBOLS (Slide 5)

Check

– Are the notes written clearly and are they easy to read?
– Are the notes short?
– Are the notes easy to understand?
– Is the logical structure of the notes clear?
– Is the main information highlighted?

B Slides for a presentation

Look at an example

1 (●14) These are the slides that Luc used to illustrate his talk. Listen to the talk and put the slides in the correct order by writing numbers 1–4 in the boxes. (One slide is missing.)

a ☐

Ideals

Faster. Higher. Stronger.
– Olympic motto

The most important thing ...
... is not to win but to take part ...
– Olympic Creed

b ☐

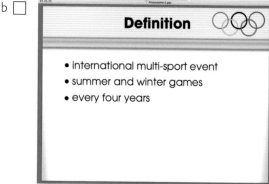

Definition

- international multi-sport event
- summer and winter games
- every four years

c ☐

History

776 BC	• first Olympics
1894	• International Olympic Committee founded
1896	• first modern Summer Olympics
1924	• first Winter Olympics

d ☐

Olympic Games

1 Introduction
2 Definition
3 History
4 Ideals
5 Symbols

2 Which section of the talk doesn't have a slide?

----

3 Which four of these things do these presentation slides include? Tick ✓ those that are included.

a bullet points and numbered lists ✓
b essential facts ☐
c single sentence quotations ☐
d full paragraph explanations ☐
e headings ☐
f more than six lines of text ☐
g lines of text that are more than eight words long ☐

4 Read these statements and (circle) the correct one.

a Presentation slides contain more information than the presenter's notes.
b Presentation slides contain less information than the presenter's notes.

Focus on ...
planning a presentation

When you are planning a presentation, divide it into three main parts.

1 **Introduction**
   – Explain who you are, what the topic of your presentation is and why it is interesting.
   – Explain how the talk is structured (e.g. *four sections*).
   – Explain when people can ask questions.

2 **Main presentation**
   – Divide your information into sections.
   – Give each section a heading.
   – Arrange your sections in a logical order.

3 **Summary**
   – Refer to the slide you used for the Introduction.
   – Briefly explain again the main part of the talk.
   – Thank the audience for their attention.

Plan a presentation for yourself.
a Decide on a topic.
b Research your topic.
c Divide your information into sections and put the points in the most logical order.

Plan

5 Look at the cue card you wrote in Exercise 10 in the first section of this unit. Is it useful to include all this information on a slide?

6 Would you include a heading like the ones you wrote in Exercises 5 and 7 in the first section of this unit?

7 Write the main heading for the slide.

Write

8 Help Luc by writing the slide notes for the Symbols section of the presentation.

Learning tip

Visual aids for presentations do not have to be scary!
- There are many computer programs that can make slides for a presentation. Some popular ones are Microsoft PowerPoint, Apple Keynote and Corel.
- If it is not possible to use computers, you could write on overhead transparencies (OHTs) and use an overhead projector (OHP).
- An alternative to slides is to write on different sheets of a flipchart and just flip the pages over during the presentation.
- Alternatively, you could use a poster, divided into sections, to illustrate your talk.

E**X**tra practice

- Write slides for the presentation you prepared for Focus on planning a presentation.
- Use the Check questions to check your slides.

Check

- Is the slide easy to understand?
- Does it include the essential facts?
- Does it have headings?
- Does it have no more than six lines of text?
- Are the lines of text shorter than eight words?

Can-do checklist

Tick what you can do.

	Can do	Need more practice
I can plan a presentation.		
I can write notes for a presentation.		
I can write slides for a presentation.		

Get ready to **write**

- Look at the leaflet and catalogue extract below and decide what the company 'Clothes Work 4U' does. Circle the best answer.
  - a They make children's clothes.
  - b They design clothes for shops.
  - c They make uniforms for companies.

- Look at the catalogue description of the Coverall (zip-up). Write the numbers (in red) of these things.
  - a prices 4
  - b colours ☐
  - c code number ☐
  - d sizes ☐

go to Useful language p. 84

We supply all your work clothing and uniform needs at competitive prices.

- T-shirts, polo shirts and work shirts
- Sweaters and jackets
- Baseball caps and hats
- Mechanics' coveralls and medical lab coats
- Restaurant and kitchen uniforms

Any garment from our extensive range can be customized with your company name and logo. We print or embroider according to your requirements and budget.

Tel: 0845 605 8652
Email: enquiries@clotheswork4u.co.uk

Clothes Work 4U, Unit 16, Barrowfield Business Park, Salisbury SP4 3TX

	CO1 Coverall (zip-up)	CO2 Coverall (button-up)
1	CO1 Coverall (zip-up)	CO2 Coverall (button-up)
2	Navy/Brown/Red	Navy/Brown/Red
3	S/M/L/XL	S/M/L/XL
4	1–10 £9.50 11+ £8.50	1–10 £9.50 11+ £8.50

TO1 T-shirt (round neck)
White/Black/Navy/Brown/Red/Green
S/L/XL
1–10 £5.00
11+ £4.50

TO2 T-shirt (v neck)
White/Black/Navy/Brown/Red/Green
S/L/XL
1–10 £5.00
11+ £4.50

HO1 Cap
White/Black/Navy/Brown/Red/Green
One size fits all
1–10 £2.00
11+ £1.50

HO2 Hat
White/Black/Navy/Brown/Red/Green
One size fits all
1–10 £2.00
11+ £1.50

Completing an order form and noting special requests

Look at an example

1 🎧**15** Darren works for Clothes Work 4U. He is taking an order from a new customer and has made two mistakes. Listen to the telephone conversation and correct the mistakes on the order form.

2 Match the standard abbreviations (a–d) with their definitions (1–4).

a L   1 as soon as possible
b "   2 the same thing
c Qty   3 large
d ASAP   4 quantity

Order form   **Clothes Work 4U**

Job No.: 0045683

Company: Easyclean	
Contact: Maureen Plumer	*URGENT*
Tel.: 020-7556-7887	*New customer (may order more), Do ASAP!*
Email: maureen@easyclean.co.uk	
Invoice address: 15a Tarpit Road, London W14 7HG	
Delivery address: "	
Design delivered: today (Print)/ Embroider	
Date required by: ASAP	

Code	Item	Colour	Size	Qty	Unit Price	Total
C02	Button-up coveralls	Navy	L	4	9.50	38.00
"	"	"	M	6	"	57.00

3 Look at the special request that Darren has written in red on the form, then decide if these statements are true (T) or false (F).

a He has put a circle round it to show that it is important. __T__
b He uses informal language. ......
c He does not use abbreviations. ......
d He explains what he wants that is unusual. ......
e He gives a reason for the request. ......

Did you know …?

Special information can be highlighted in many ways. For example, by putting the word *Special* or N.B. (from the Latin *nota bene* = note well) in front of the information.

Plan

4 Write the word that Darren uses to show that the thing needs to be done quickly.

----

5 Look at some ways of shortening and emphasizing the importance of the information.

Long sentence   **Shortened sentence**

a This is a new customer *who* may order more.   New customer (may order more)

   ↑   ↑   ↑   ↑

Important information   *Who* introduces extra information   Put important information at the front to emphasize it   Brackets ( ) surround extra information

b You should do them as soon as possible!   Do   ASAP!

Put the verb at the front to emphasize it   Abbreviation

6 Shorten these sentences by crossing out information that is not useful. <u>Underline</u> essential information and put brackets ( ) around useful extra information.

a ~~Please~~ do ~~the~~ <u>coveralls</u> in <u>olive green</u> (to match the colour of ~~our~~ vans and trucks).
b We have some larger people working for us. We need T-shirts in XXL.
c Can you do long-sleeve not short-sleeve T-shirts, please?
d Please treat these coveralls with chemicals to make them flame-proof. They are for fire safety officers.
e We also need bags in the same design.

7 Rewrite your answers from Exercise 6 as notes on order forms. Make sure that you put the most important information at the front to emphasize it.

a Do coveralls in olive green (to match trucks)

Write

8 Look at the business card of one of Clothes Work 4U's regular customers.

🔊 16 Fabio has left a message on the Clothes Work 4U answer machine. Listen to the message and complete the order form below. Add any special requests. (You can listen to the message more than once. You will need to look in the catalogue on page 66 to find the prices and one of the codes.)

Fabio Lopez
Marketing Executive

WGL Technology
Redgate House
Ipswich
IP24 2HC
Tel 01842 763074

Order form — Clothes Work 4U

Job No.: 0045684							

Company:

Contact:

Tel.:

Email:

Invoice address:

Delivery address:

Design delivered: | Print / Embroider

Date required by:

Code	Item		Colour	Size	Qty	Unit Price	Total

Check

- Have you completed all the necessary boxes on the form?
- Have you used ditto marks (") appropriately?
- Have you made a note of the special request?
- Is your note easy to understand?
- Does your note explain what you want your colleague to do and why?
- Does your note stand out on the form? That is: Have you circled it or highlighted it?

E X tra practice

1 🔊 17 Fabio has phoned back. He wants to change his order. Listen to the recording and change the order form.
2 Add a new note to explain why the order form has been changed.
3 Use the Check questions to check you have done everything.

Class bonus

- Practise completing order forms and noting special requests with another student.
- Use your company's catalogue or find a catalogue or webpage that you use to choose products. Look at the same page together and write down possible special requests for products on that page.
- Sit back-to-back or phone each other from different rooms. One student is the customer and the other student is the supplier. The supplier must complete the order form on the right.
- At the end, check that you have got the order right and made a note of the special request. Use the Check questions to help you.

Order form

Job No.: 008347							

Company:

Contact:

Tel.:

Email:

Invoice address:

Delivery address:

Date required by:

Code	Item		Colour	Size	Qty	Unit Price	Total

Focus on ...
silent consonants and double consonants

18 Listen to how the words below are pronounced. The red consonants in these consonant pairs are silent and it is easy to forget them when spelling these words.

wh	wr	kn	ght	ck or ck	lk / lf / ld	gn	mb	st
why	write	know	right	black	talk, half, could	design	comb	listen

1 Look at how we spell the words below. Put them in the correct place in the table above. (It may be possible to put some words in more than one box.)
calf   daughter   foreign   knife   quick   thumb   whistle   white   would   wrong

2 **19** Listen to check how the words are pronounced.

3 Each of these sentences has a silent letter spelling mistake. Correct the mistakes.

a I would be grateful if you could contact me as soon as possible.

b When you get to the office, nock on the door and walk straight in.

c The plane is about to land, please fasen your seat belt.

d Wich type of shirt do you want to order?

e The plumer couldn't repair the toilet.

f I'm afraid you sent the rong thing.

People often make spelling mistakes with double consonants. Look at these common words with double consonants.
a**cc**o**mm**odation   begi**nn**ing   impo**ss**ible   rea**ll**y   a**dd**re**ss** (Be careful: double **d** and double **s**)   busine**ss** (Be careful: double **s** at the end only)
Be careful! At the end of words, *full* has only one **l**. For example: *beautiful, careful.*

4 Look at this email from one of the Clothes Work 4U's satisfied customers. They forgot to use their spell-checker. Find five double-consonant mistakes and correct them.

Clothes Work 4U are great. In the past we found it dificult to buy good work clothes but since we've been doing busines with you we've had no problems! Your staff are realy helpfull. Nothing seems imposible for them!

Did you know ...?
Silent letters cause many spelling problems in English! There are a lot of words in English with silent letters. For example: *address, colour, know*, etc. This is because their pronunciation has changed over hundreds of years but their spelling has not changed. In the 1800s an American, Noah Webster, tried to solve this problem. He wrote a dictionary that made the spelling of many words simpler. This is why Americans spell some words differently to British people (for example: *color*).

Can-do checklist
Tick what you can do.

	Can do	Need more practice
I can complete an order form correctly.		
I can note special requests.		
I can use ditto marks (") appropriately.		
I can use some spelling patterns for words that contain silent consonants.		

Get ready to write

- What do you think the woman in the photograph is doing?

- What kind of machine is she using? Circle the correct answer.

  a hammer   b drill   c scissors

- Read this email and underline:

  a Jill's problem

  b what she wants First Engineering to do.

From: Jill Lawrie, EKF Furniture Workshop
Date: 23 February
To: enquiries@firstengineering.com.hk
Subject: Enquiry

I was wondering if you could help me. In our workshop, we use a TX8745 drill (made by Telford Drills Ltd in 1992). Unfortunately, it has broken and Telford Drills no longer sell parts for this model. Please advise if it is possible for you to make a part.

An early answer would be very much appreciated. Thank you for your help.

- What do you think First Engineering will do next?

go to Useful language p. 84

Replying to an enquiry

Look at an example

1 **Christine Kee Yung at First Engineering has replied to Jill. This is the email she sent her. Can Christine help Jill?**

2 **Look at the email again and put these things in the order they appear.**

   a Christine explains that she has attached something. ☐

   b Christine thanks Jill for her enquiry. ☐1

   c Christine answers Jill's questions. ☐

   d Christine explains what Jill should do next. ☐

From: christine@firstengineering.com.hk
Date: 23 February
To: Jill Lawrie, EKF Furniture Workshop
Subject: Re: Enquiry
Attachments: brochure.pdf

Dear Ms Lawrie,

Thank you for your enquiry about our engineering services. I have pleasure in attaching a brochure.

As you will see, we do all kinds of engineering work from large projects to making small, individual items, so your drill part should not pose a problem. I would be happy to discuss your specific requirements. Please feel free to contact me direct on +852 2861 7273.

I look forward to hearing from you.

Best regards,
Christine Kee Yung

3 Look at these expressions from Christine's email.

> Thank you for …
> I have pleasure in …
> I would be happy to …

Find another polite expression in her email and complete this sentence.

I look _____

_____

4 Look at *Appendix 5 Think about style 1* on page 89. Then replace these friendly and informal expressions with more polite and formal expressions from Christine's email.

a Thanks

Thank you for your enquiry ...

b Here's a brochure

_____

_____

c It shouldn't be a problem

_____

_____

d I'll talk to you about it

_____

_____

e Phone me

_____

_____

Focus on …
punctuation and capital letters

Look at *Appendix 9 Punctuation* on page 93.

1 Look at this part of an email. Put full stops and capital letters in the correct places.

> Y
> your school, the a1 business school, was recommended by a friend
>
> i would be grateful if you could help me my company is interested in
>
> developing some of its workers' english language skills

2 Correct the punctuation and use of capital letters in these sentences. Sometimes you will need to add punctuation.
  a Can you come to a meeting on either tomorrow, friday or saturday?
  b The cost is £3,69 per item.
  c Please send a catalogue?
  d My brother steve, is a mechanic.
  e NB send 500 brochures today!
  f We sent 35.000 brochures yesterday.
  g If you want to please come to the meeting.
  h I'm afraid I cant help you with your enquiry.
  i My companys' head office is in oslo.
  j After you have spoken to him please let me know.

Plan

5 **Use the expressions in the box to complete these sentences. (More than one answer may be possible.)**

> 1 your requirements 2 ~~your enquiry~~ 3 a quote/quotation
> 4 your letter 5 a brochure

  a Thank you for _____ your enquiry _____
  b I am pleased to enclose _____
  c I have pleasure in attaching _____
  d I would be happy to send _____
  e Please feel free to phone me to discuss _____

Did you know …?

Business emails and letters are very similar but they do have some differences.

Letter
Dear …, / Yours …,
Opening/closing phrases are compulsory.
enclose a brochure/document/picture

Email
Opening/closing phrases are optional.
attach a document/picture/brochure/PDF file

Learning tip

Try to make your writing more interesting. There can be many ways of saying the same thing. Try not to use the same phrase more than once in a paragraph.

OK: Thank you for your enquiry about our stationery. We sell *all kinds of* paper and *all kinds of* pens.

Better: Thank you for your enquiry about our stationery. We sell *all kinds of* paper and *a variety of* pens.

6 Look at these expressions. Most of them mean the same thing. Circle the expression which does NOT mean the same thing as the others.

a all kinds of   b a variety of   c a wide range of
d a few   e all types of

7 Complete these sentences. Use the pictures and the words in brackets to help you.

a As you will see, we repair all kinds of bicycles. (repair)

b As you will see, _____ (fix)

c As you _____ (supply)

d As _____ (sell)

8 You work for the marketing department of the A1 Business School. Your boss has given you this email and note. He wants you to reply to Alexi. Use the information in the email and note to complete sentences a–d.

From: alexi@romanovnet.ru
Date: 7 May
To: A1 Business School
Subject: **English course**

Your school was recommended by a business associate. I would be grateful if you could help me. My company is interested in developing some of its employees' English language skills. Please advise if you could design a 5-day course specific to our needs, the cost and the number of hours' tuition you would provide per week. Many thanks for your help.

· Cost: £1,000 / employee
· 30 hours / one week
· Send 'custom-made courses' brochure (shows the courses we do)

a Thank you for your <u>email/enquiry</u> about our
   _____ .
b I have pleasure in attaching a _____ .
c As you will see, _____ so designing a
   course for you should not pose a problem.
d The cost would be _____ for a course of
   _____ hours.

Write

9 Use your answers from Exercise 8 to write an email replying to Alexi's enquiry.

Check

– Does your email make sense?
– Have you thanked the person for their enquiry?
– Have you explained that you have attached something?
– Have you answered any questions (for example about the cost and length of the course)?
– Have you explained what you would like the person to do?
– Have you written in a more polite and formal style?
– Have you checked for spelling, capitalization and punctuation mistakes?

Focus on ...
common spelling mistakes

Farouk

Farouk has written this email to a tour company.

I saw ¹your ²advertisment in the April issue of *Places to go* magazine. I am very ³intrested in visiting ⁴diffrent ⁵countries and learning about ⁶thier famous places too. ⁷Unfortunatly, I cannot travel far ⁸becaus I am ⁹scared of flying. Your coach ¹⁰holydays sound excellent. I ¹¹belive you run some trips to Italy. Can you tell me if this trip is ¹²avaliable in ¹³February? I am just a ¹⁴littel ¹⁵worried about how ¹⁶confortable the coaches are. ¹⁷Plese ¹⁸right back and let me know. I would also be ¹⁹gratefull if you ²⁰coud send a brochure.

1 He has made fifteen spelling mistakes. Help him to correct the email. Look at the underlined words and decide if they are correct ✓ or incorrect ✗.

1 ✓ 2 ☐ 3 ☐ 4 ☐ 5 ☐ 6 ☐ 7 ☐
8 ☐ 9 ☐ 10 ☐ 11 ☐ 12 ☐ 13 ☐ 14 ☐
15 ☐ 16 ☐ 17 ☐ 18 ☐ 19 ☐ 20 ☐

2 Write the correct spellings of the words Farouk has spelt wrong. Use a dictionary to help you.

3 Look at some pieces of writing you have done recently. Make a note of five spelling mistakes that you often make.

4 Look at *Appendix 8 Spelling* on page 92. Decide which idea for learning spellings is best for each of your five words. Try learning them that way and then test yourself after two hours, four hours and 24 hours.

Extra practice

– You have received this email at work. (If you do not work, search on the Internet for a company you are interested in. Imagine you work for them.)

> Please advise if you can customize your product or service to meet my company's needs.

– Write an email in reply.
– Use the Check questions to check your email.
– Ask your teacher or an English-speaking friend to check that you have answered all points of the enquiry and that your email is logically ordered.

Class bonus

– In groups, write one list of ten words that you have difficulty in spelling. (You may want to use a dictionary to help you find the correct spelling!)
– Write ten sentences. Each sentence must include one of the words on your list spelt incorrectly.
– Swap your ten sentences with another group.
– Try to find and correct the ten spelling mistakes on your new list.
– After five minutes, swap back. Give the other group a mark (out of ten) for the corrections of your original errors.
– The winner is the group with most correct marks!

Can-do checklist

Tick what you can do.

	Can do	Need more practice
I can reply to an enquiry.		
I can find and correct punctuation mistakes and capital letters.		
I can find and correct common spelling mistakes.		
I can choose the best way to learn spellings I regularly get wrong.		

Unit 16
Can you make the 17th?

Get ready to *write*

1

2

○ Look at pictures 1 and 2. What do you think VOCSCRIBE does? Circle the best answer.
   a It helps you design websites.
   b It types text for you when you speak.
   c It gives you free phonecalls.

○ Answer these questions.
   a Have you used a product similar to VOCSCRIBE?
   b Would you be interested in buying it?
   c Which of the box designs do you prefer?

Martin Frohlich is personal assistant to the managing director of the company that makes VOCSCRIBE. When he arrived at work this morning, he found a message on his answerphone.

○ 🎧 20 Listen to the message and answer the question. *What does the managing director want Martin to do?* Circle the best answer.
   a arrange a meeting for next week
   b finalize the box design
   c finalize the marketing campaign

go to Useful language p. 84

A An email arranging a meeting

Look at an example

1 **Look at the email Martin wrote. Write the expressions from the email that do these things.**

a greet someone
   Dear Vocscribe team,

b explain why Martin is emailing
   ----

c invite someone to a meeting
   ----

d explain what will happen at the meeting
   ----

e ask for something
   ----

f end the email

From: Martin Frohlich
Date: 29 April 10.24
To: c.lopez@vcsoftsol.com; m.johnson@vcsoftsol.com; m.muller@vcsoftsol.com; y.lei@vcsoftsol.com
cc: Yuki Okowa
Subject: **Vocscribe meeting**

Dear Vocscribe team,

Yuki has asked me to contact you and arrange a meeting for next week. She would like to invite you all to meet here at the Peabody Building on Monday at 9.30 a.m.

The main focus of discussion will be how to promote the product.

Here is a draft agenda:

> 1. Packaging (box design, image for website, etc.)
> 2. Marketing (style/media/same campaign in all countries?)
> 3. A.O.B.

Please advise me by 5 p.m. if you can attend or if you would like to add anything to the agenda.

Regards,

Martin Frohlich
P.A. to Ms Yuki Okowa, M.D.
VCSoftSol, Inc.
The Peabody Building
London WC1B 7PH

Tel: + 44 (0)121 732 5374 (direct line)
Fax: + 44 (0)121 732 5301
http://uk:vcsoftsol.com/

2 Find the short form of these expressions in the email on page 74.

a any other business .A..O..B...
b at (*in email addresses*) ....
c copy sent to ....
d personal assistant ....
e managing director ....

3 Martin's email is polite and formal because he does not know all the people he is writing to. <u>Underline</u> the polite and formal expressions in his email that mean the same as these less formal words.

a email, phone or write to you
b tell
c come to / make a meeting

Plan

4 Decide if these expressions are more suitable to use in an email to a colleague you do not know very well or a colleague you *do* know well. Write them in the correct places in the chart below.

I need an answer …
~~Dear colleague,~~
I would be grateful if you could reply …
Just to let you know …
Would you like to come to …?

I'm emailing you to invite you …
Best regards,
Best wishes,
Would you like to attend …?
Dear Martin,

What do you write …	… to a colleague that you don't know well?	… to a colleague you do know well?
to greet someone?	a Dear colleague,	b
to explain the reason for the email?	c	d
to make an invitation?	e	f
to ask for a response?	g	h
to close the email?	i	j

5 Look at this notice from the company's noticeboard. What are the staff invited to?

Invitation to all staff

Communication Training Session
Making your voice heard in a noisy world

This course will help you to understand:
What you want to say
How to say it appropriately
How to check someone's really listening

Tuesday 12 May, 16.00 – 17.00
at the New Meeting Room
Trainer: Sheila Peacock
Please note that the room is quite small,
so there are limited spaces.

6 A colleague of yours is going to email everyone in the company about the training course. What is wrong with her email?

Hi everyone,

Nice weather today. We're having a training session. Yuki thinks we don't communicate very well. It's some time next week. Do you think you can make it? There's only a few places.

Bye,
Sheila

7 Read the email and notice again and answer the questions.

a <u>Underline</u> four pieces of information in the notice that are missing from the email.
b What piece of information in the email could be cut? <u>Underline</u> it.
c Do you think the information in the email is in the best order?
d Is the language appropriate for the reader? Do you think it is polite and formal enough?
e Does the reader know what they should do next?

Write

8 Use the answers to Exercises 7 and 8 to help you rewrite the email for your colleague.

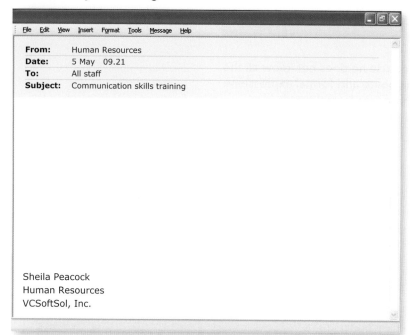

From: Human Resources
Date: 5 May 09.21
To: All staff
Subject: Communication skills training

Sheila Peacock
Human Resources
VCSoftSol, Inc.

Check

- Does your email answer these questions?
  Why is the writer emailing people?
  What is the training course or event about?
  When and where is it?
  How and when should the reader apply for the course?
- Does it answer the questions in the best order?
- Is the language appropriate for the reader?

B An email confirming arrangements

Look at an example

1 Look at the email Martin Frohlich sent confirming the arrangements for the meeting. Find and write the answers to these questions.

a What is the email about?

----

b When is the meeting being held?

----

c Where is it being held?

From: Martin Frohlich
Date: 30 April 11.45
To: c.lopez@vcsoftsol.com; m.johnson@vcsoftsol.com; m.muller@vcsoftsol.com; y.lei@vcsoftsol.com
cc: Yuki Okowa
Subject: Vocscribe meeting

Dear Vocscribe team,

Thank you for your prompt responses. I am happy to confirm that everyone can attend the meeting at the Peabody Building on Monday at 9.30 a.m. It will be held in the New Meeting Room and will finish by 11 a.m.

I will look forward to seeing you on Monday.

Regards,

Martin Frohlich

P.A. to Ms Yuki Okowa, M.D.
VCSoftSol, Inc.
The Peabody Building
London WC1B 7PH

Tel: + 44 (0)121 732 5374 (direct line)
Fax: + 44 (0)121 732 5301
http://uk:vcsoftsol.com/

2 <u>Underline</u> a more polite and formal word in Martin's email that means *speedy*.

3 Write the expression that Martin uses to say that the meeting is definitely going to happen.

----

4 <u>Underline</u> the sentence that gives new information (that is, information which is not in the email on page 74).

5 Write the expression that Martin uses to say that he will also be at the meeting.

Plan

6 Look at the email you wrote in Section A, Exercise 9. Write the answers to these questions about the meeting.

   a What is it about? ----------------------------

   b When is it being held? ---------------------------

   c Where is it being held? ---------------------------

7 Sheila Peacock has asked you to write an email to the trainees. She has also left this note on your desk.

> Can you organize refreshments for the training session? Just a few cakes and some hot drinks will do.
> Thanks,
> Sheila

Write a sentence that you can include in your email giving information about refreshments.

Write

8 Write the email to a trainee confirming their place. Use your answers from Exercises 6 and 7 to help you.

Check

– Does your email answer these questions?
  Why are you emailing the person?
  When and where is the training course?
– Have you told the trainee about the refreshments?
– Is the language appropriate for the reader?

Can-do checklist

Tick what you can do.

	Can do	Need more practice
I can write emails inviting people to a meeting.		
I can write emails to confirm arrangements.		
I can order information logically in an email.		
I can check that my language is appropriate for the reader.		

Review 2
Units 9–16

Choose one answer for each question.

A Planning your writing

Choosing what to write

1 You have been asked by your teacher to write about global warming. What do you do?

  a complete a form   b write a message
  c write a letter or email   d write a description

2 You have been asked by your teacher to give a talk explaining global warming. What do you do?

  a complete a form   b write notes
  c write a letter or email   d write a description

3 You want to get an old sofa repaired. You want to find out if a company can help you. What do you do?

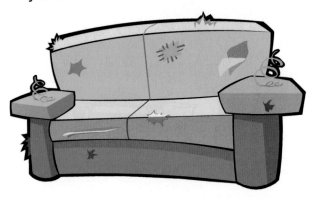

  a complete a form   b write notes
  c write a letter or email   d write a description

4 A company wants to find out what you think about its products. What do they ask you to do?

  a complete a form   b write notes
  c write a letter or email   d write a description

Knowing the reader

5 You are writing an email to a colleague you know well. How formal will your email be?

  a friendly and informal   b polite and formal

6 You are writing an email to a large team of colleagues, some of whom you do not know. How formal will your email be?

  a friendly and informal   b polite and formal

Choosing information

7 Which of these things would you not include in your notes for the introduction of a presentation?

  a how the talk is structured
  b a reminder to greet the audience
  c a reminder to explain when the audience can ask questions
  d a lot of detailed facts

8 What would you put in this box on an order form?

Item

  a The quantity of things that the customer wants to order.
  b The name of the thing that the customer wants to order.
  c The price of the thing that the customer wants to order.
  d The colour of the thing that the customer wants to order.

9 You want to make notes about a country. Which of these sources will probably give the most neutral information?

  a the country's tourism website
  b an encyclopedia

B Check

Checking that the reader has enough information

10 Read this part of an order form. What information is missing that the reader needs to know?

Code	Item	Colour	Size	Qty	Unit Price	Total
S02	Sweater	Red	L	4	9.50	38.00
	Trousers	"	"	"	7.50	30.00

a What colour?   b How big?   c Exactly what?
d How many?

11 You are making notes from a book on the history of popular music. What information could be cut?

Blues is simple: full of emotion and power, based on three key chords (E, A and B7) normally played in a 12 bar structure. It took its name from the distinctive blue notes used in African work songs, notes played or sung at a slightly lower pitch than normal. At its heart, it was a democratic music: almost anyone could play or sing it. The instruments were simple, too: guitars, harmonicas … things that were cheap and easy to carry.

a text in red
b text in pink
c text in green
d text in blue

Checking that information is well organized

12 Hsei is writing a reply to an enquiry. In which of these paragraphs is the information best organized?

a

Re: Your email of 27 June
Thank you for your enquiry. I have pleasure in enclosing a brochure. Please feel free to contact me direct.

b

I have pleasure in enclosing a brochure. Please feel free to contact me direct. Thank you for your enquiry.
Re: Your email of 27 June

c

Re: Your email of 27 June
Please feel free to contact me direct. Thank you for your enquiry. I have pleasure in enclosing a brochure.

d

Re: Your email of 27 June
Thank you for your enquiry. Please feel free to contact me direct. I have pleasure in enclosing a brochure.

13 **Which of these is the best organized presentation slide?**

a

Music in the early 1950s

'Crooners'
Bing Crosby/Frank Sinatra

Blues
BB King/Muddy Waters

First rock song
Bill Haley & the Comets (1953)
— *Crazy, man, crazy*

b

Music in the early 1950s

- Bing Crosby and Frank Sinatra 'crooned' to very controlled white middle-class audiences.
- BB King and Muddy Waters used electric guitars and developed the Blues.
- Bill Haley and the Comets had the first rock song in the American charts in 1953. It was called *Crazy, man, crazy*.

c

Music in the early 1950s

- Bing Crosby/Frank Sinatra
- BB King/Muddy Waters
- Bill Haley & the Comets

d

Music in the early 1950s

Music in the 1950s developed out of jazz, crooning, blues and Country and Western. Bing Crosby and Frank Sinatra 'crooned' to very controlled white middle-class audiences. BB King and Muddy Waters used electric guitars and developed the Blues. Bill Haley and the Comets had the first rock song in the American charts in 1953. It was called *Crazy, man, crazy*.

Checking style

14 **Federico is writing to invite a colleague he has never met to a meeting. Which is the best way of inviting her?**

a Would you like to come to a meeting on 16 August?
b I am emailing you to invite you to a meeting on 16 August.
c How about coming to a meeting on 16 August?
d Please come to a meeting on 16 August.

15 **You are writing to a company for the first time. Rewrite this request so it is more polite and formal.**

Can you send a brochure? ....

....

Checking punctuation

16 **Which of these sentences uses an incorrect capital letter or full stop?**

a This is to confirm that I can make the meeting on 21 June.
b N.B. You need to apply for a place on the course.
c Please email the Price to Mr Henderson.
d Tell him I'll see him tomorrow.

17 **Rewrite this note. Correct the spelling and use of capital letters.**

Nb they want to order 15 shirts. 6 pairs of trousers and 5 pairs of Gloves.

....
....
....
....

18 a

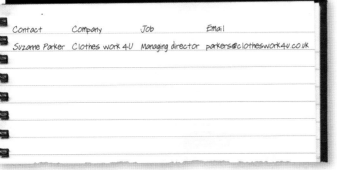

Suzanne Parker
Managing Director

Clothes Work 4U
Unit 16 Barrowfield Business Park
Salisbury
SP4 3TX
Tel: 0845 6058650 Email: parkers@clotheswork4u.co.uk

b

Darren Hall
Sales Executive

Clothes Work 4U
Unit 16 Barrowfield Business Park
Salisbury
SP4 3TX
Tel: 0845 6058652 Email: enquiries@clotheswork4u.co.uk

Contact	Company	Job	Email
Suzanne Parker	Clothes work 4U	Managing director	parkers@clotheswork4u.co.uk

Add Darren Hall's details to your list of contacts. Use ditto marks (") where you can.

Checking grammar

19 **Your boss has asked you to write a description for a staff handbook. The handbook will explain how to deal with paperwork in the company. Choose the best sentence to use.**

a I complete a form, place it in a folder and file it under today's date.
b Each form is completed, placed in a folder and filed under that day's date.

20 **Which of these sentences is correct?**

a Industrial development makes people richer. But also increases pollution.
b Although industrial development makes people richer, it also increases pollution.
c Even if industrial development makes people richer. It also increases pollution.
d Industrial development makes people richer, however, it also increases pollution.

21 **Which of these sentences is correct?**

a The Chinese invented rockets. Many years later, the Americans landed on the moon.
b The Chinese invented rockets. After, the Americans landed on the moon.
c The Americans landed on the moon. Many years later, the Chinese invented rockets.
d After the Chinese invented rockets. The Americans landed on the moon.

22 **Which of these expressions best emphasizes what must be done?**

a Phone ASAP!
b Please phone her
c New customer (please phone)
d New customer who you need to phone

Checking vocabulary

23 **Maria is writing a letter. She can't remember the correct word to complete this sentence. Choose the correct word for her.**

Thank you for your enquiry. I have pleasure in … a brochure.

a attaching
b enclosing
c putting in
d sending

Checking spelling

24 **Which of these green words has a silent letter missing?**

a Could you check the spelling in this letter?
b Do you now your postcode?
c Please write clearly.
d Listen carefully to voicemail messages.

25 **Which of these sentences has a double letter spelling mistake?**

a I really love folk music.
b Dictionaries can be very usefull.
c English spelling is impossible!
d Student accommodation is not included in the course fees.

Appendix 1
Useful language

This section contains a list of words and expressions that are used in the texts in different units. These words and expressions are not normally essential for the writing task but they will help you to understand what you are being asked to do.

You may want to look at the list before you begin the unit and circle any new words and expressions. As you find them in the unit, you can try to guess their meaning. When you have finished you can look at the list and check that you understand the words and expressions.

Alternatively, you can look at the list of words and expressions before you begin the unit and look up any new ones in a dictionary.

You can also adapt the list to help your own learning. For new words, write a translation into your own language and an example sentence in English.

Unit 1

proceed *verb* ....
solar *adjective* ....
battery *noun* ....
recharge (a battery) *verb* ....
order (something) *verb* ....
account *noun* ....
confirm (something) *verb* ....
password *noun* ....
cardholder *noun* ....
valid *adjective* ....
expire *verb* ....
shopping basket (UK)/cart (US) *noun* ....
shipping (US)/delivery (UK) address *noun phrase* ....
optional *adjective* ....
billing (US)/invoice (UK) address *noun phrase* ....
zip code (US) *noun* ....
postcode (UK) *noun* ....
payment method *noun* ....
expiration date *noun phrase* ....
expiry date *noun phrase* ....
checkout *noun* ....

Unit 2

book/reserve (something) *verb* ....
round trip ≠ one way *noun phrase* ....
go to/depart from *verb* ....
select (something) *verb* ....
country of residence *noun* ....

destination *noun* ....
preference *noun* ....
aisle seat ≠ window seat *noun phrase* ....
destination *noun* ....
verify *verb* ....
economy/standard/premium *adjective*

pick (something) up ≠ drop (something) off *verb*

return (something) *verb* ....
satellite navigation *compound noun* ....
automatic/manual transmission *compound noun*

Unit 3

landing card *noun* ....
application *noun* ....
visa *noun* ....
waiver *noun* ....
country of citizenship *noun phrase* ....
temporary/permanent ....
official *noun* ....
occupation *noun* ....
mature *adjective* ....
term *noun phrase* ....
spam *noun* ....
part-time/full-time *adjective* ....
employed *adjective* ....
block capitals *noun phrase* ....
syllable *noun* ....

Unit 4

accomodation *noun* ....
run (something) *verb* ....
availability *noun* ....
double (room) *noun phrase* ....
en suite (room) *noun phrase* ....
hot spring *noun phrase* ....
hospitality *noun* ....
tariff *noun* ....
book (something) *verb* ....
per person *noun phrase* ....
deposit *noun* ....
secure (something) *verb* ....
confirmation *noun* ....
charge *verb* ....

Unit 5

takeaway meal *compound noun* _____
ready-meal *compound noun* _____
microwave meal *compound noun* _____
ingredients *noun* _____
reheat *verb* _____
step *noun* _____
separate (something) from (something) *verb*

_____
whisk *verb* _____

Unit 6

text (someone) *verb* _____
symbols *noun* _____
abbreviations *noun* _____
keypad *noun* _____
predictive text *noun* _____
standard *adjective* _____
essential *adjective* _____
exchange *noun* _____
online *adjective* _____
emphasize *verb* _____
emoticon *noun* _____

Unit 7

keep in touch (with someone) *verb* _____
catch up (with things) *verb* _____
accountant *noun* _____
global warming *noun phrase* _____
news *pl noun* _____
donut (US) (UK: doughnut) *noun* _____
celebrate *verb* _____
celebration *noun* _____
band *noun* _____
pen friend *noun* _____
remind someone (about something) *verb* _____
break down *verb* _____
contraction *noun* _____
possession *noun* _____
annual *adjective* _____
service *noun* _____
litter *noun* _____

Unit 8

weblog/blog *noun* _____
journal *noun* _____
scary *adjective* _____
ride *noun* _____
autograph *noun* _____
rollercoaster *compound noun* _____

top tip *noun phrase* _____
save (someone from doing something) *verb* _____
comment *noun* _____
entry (in a journal) *noun* _____
post (an entry/comment) *verb* _____
blogger *noun* _____
surf *verb* _____
shut (something) *verb* _____
cage *noun* _____
rare *adjective* _____
breed *verb* _____
the wild *noun phrase* _____
support *verb* _____

Unit 9

borrow *verb* _____
issues desk *compound noun* _____
feedback *noun* _____
evaluation *noun* _____
reputation *noun* _____
facility *noun* _____
tutor *noun* _____
tutorial *noun* _____
satisfied *adjective* _____
grade (something) *verb* _____
rank (something) *verb* _____
recommend *verb* _____
recommendation *noun* _____

Unit 10

choir *noun* _____
prominence *noun* _____
prolific *adjective* _____
harmony *noun* _____
national treasure *noun phrase* _____
collaboration *noun* _____
output *noun* _____
cheesy *adjective* _____
jumble *noun* _____
cover (of a record) *noun* _____
ruin *verb* _____
soulful *adjective* _____
point of view *noun phrase* _____
lyrics *pl noun* _____
boycott *noun* _____
audience *noun* _____
apartheid *noun* _____
abolish something *verb* _____
inauguration *noun* _____
source *noun* _____

Unit 11

farm labourer *compound noun* _____
poppy *noun* _____
childhood *noun* _____
event *noun* _____
background *noun* _____
battlefield *noun* _____
symbol *noun* _____
symbolism *noun* _____
first *noun* _____
represent *verb* _____
invent (something) *verb* _____
emergency *noun* _____
commit a crime *verb* _____
forbidden *adjective* _____

Unit 12

wind turbine *compound noun* _____
continent *noun* _____
blade *noun* _____
cable *noun* _____
generator *noun* _____
tower *noun* _____
energy *noun* _____
revolutions *noun* _____
produce (something) *verb* _____
wind-power *noun* _____
power (something) *verb* _____
gear *noun* _____
process *noun* _____
generate (electricity) *verb* _____
electricity grid *compound noun* _____
store *noun* _____
the developing world *noun* _____
torch *noun* _____
wind *verb* _____
solar-powered *adjective* _____

Unit 13

represent *verb* _____
presentation/talk *noun* _____
screen *noun* _____
definition *noun* _____
symbol *noun* _____
section *noun* _____
audience *noun* _____
summary *noun* _____
key points/facts *noun* _____
visual aids *noun* _____
venue *noun* _____
light *verb* _____
symbolize *verb* _____

link *noun* _____
generation *noun* _____
flag *noun* _____
link *verb* _____
motto *noun* _____
quotation *noun* _____

Unit 14

uniform *noun* _____
coverall *noun* _____
customize (something) *verb* _____
polo shirt *compound noun* _____
sweater *noun* _____
jacket *noun* _____
baseball cap *compound noun* _____
lab coat *compound noun* _____
extensive *adjective* _____
range *noun* _____
logo *noun* _____
code *noun* _____
item *noun* _____
embroider *verb* _____
zip (something) up *verb* _____
button (something) up *verb* _____
chemical *noun* _____
flame-proof *adjective* _____
customer *noun* _____

Unit 15

enquiry *noun* _____
wonder *verb* _____
drill *noun* _____
attachment *noun* _____
requirement *noun* _____
pose a problem *verb* _____
brochure *noun* _____
quote/quotation *noun* _____
enclose *verb* _____
tuition *noun* _____

Unit 16

personal assistant *compound noun* _____
finalize (something) *verb* _____
marketing campaign *compound noun* _____
focus *noun* _____
draft *noun* _____
agenda *noun* _____
greet *verb* _____
appropriately *adverb* _____
prompt *adjective* _____
refreshments *noun* _____

Appendix 2
What can I improve?

What do I want to do?

Do I want to ...		Go to Unit ...
complete personal forms?	→	1, 2, 3
write personal emails and letters?	→	4, 7
leave messages and instructions?	→	5
send personal SMS / text messages?	→	6
write IM (instant messages)?	→	6
write a blog?	→	8
add comments to a blog?	→	8
take notes from a talk?	→	9
complete feedback forms?	→	9
make notes from the Internet, books and magazines?	→	10
write a personal story?	→	11
describe a business or scientific process?	→	12
make notes and slides for a presentation?	→	13
complete an order form and note special requests?	→	14
reply to an enquiry?	→	15
arrange a meeting, invite people and confirm arrangements?	→	16

How good is my writing?

Can I ...		No / Not sure		How important is this to me? (1= very important, 5 = not important)		Go to Unit(s) ...
predict what information an online form will ask me to complete?			→		→	2
check new sources of information for opinions and facts?			→		→	10
order information logically?			→		→	13, 16
edit for essential information?			→		→	6, 13
link similar things using *and, also, too/as well* and *as well as*?			→		→	5
link positive and negative comments using *but, however, even if* and *although*?			→		→	9
emphasize how two important steps are linked using *before* and *after*?			→		→	5
use sequencers (e.g. *First, Then, Next*, etc.)?			→		→	5
use time sequencers (e.g. *Later/Then/Afterwards*, etc.)?			→		→	11
use *as, since* and *so* to link reasons and results?			→		→	4
link ideas and thoughts?			→		→	12

Can I …	No / Not sure		How important is this to me? (1= very important, 5 = not important)		Go to Unit(s) …
write for a specific reader?		→		→	8, 11, 16
spell plurals correctly?		→		→	1
spell words which have double consonants?		→		→	14
spell words which contain the most common silent letters?		→		→	14
spell /eɪ/ words correctly?		→		→	3
find and correct common spelling mistakes?		→		→	15
use apostrophes correctly?		→		→	7
use ditto marks (") appropriately?		→		→	14
use punctuation to make notes easier to understand?		→		→	9
find and correct capital letter and punctuation mistakes?		→		→	15
use symbols and abbreviations in notes?		→		→	10
indicate a preference on a form (e.g. *If…, tick here.* □)?		→		→	3
write my own news and comment on other people's news?		→		→	7
write headlines?		→		→	8
use symbolism to give extra meaning?		→		→	11
use present simple passive forms?		→		→	12

Appendix 3
Check your writing

Planning

Think about these questions when you are writing.

Why am I writing?
Who is the reader going to be?
What am I writing about?
What information does the reader need?
What does the reader know about this subject already?
Will diagrams or illustrations help them to understand?
What type of writing should I use?

First check questions

Use these questions to check your writing.

Communication
Does the reader understand why I am writing to them?

Information
Have I included all the information that the reader needs?
Have I included any information that is not useful for the reader?
Have I repeated any information?

Organization
Have I organized my ideas and information logically?
Have I linked sentences together?
Is it easy to understand what the pronouns refer to?

Layout and style
Is this a letter? Have I put everything in the right place on the page?
Have I put the information into paragraphs? Have I put spaces between the paragraphs?
Is the writing personal, informal or formal? Is this the correct style for this reader?

Second check questions

Use these questions to check the accuracy of your language.

Punctuation
Does the punctuation make the writing easy to understand?
Have I used a comma when I need a full stop?
Have I used an exclamation mark when I need a full stop?
Have I used apostrophes in contractions and to show possession?

Grammar
Have I used the correct verb form?
Do the subject and verb agree in each sentence? Is the subject missing?
Are the words in the right order?
Have I used the right prepositions?
Have I checked the nouns?
Are they uncountable? Are they plural?
Have I used the right article?

Capital letters
Have I used capital letters in the right place?

Vocabulary
Have I used the right word?
Can I use a specific word not a general one?
Is the word too weak or too strong?

Spelling
Have I checked difficult words are spelt correctly?
Have I checked words that I often get wrong? e.g. *to/two/too*?
If I am using a spell-checker, have I also checked for meaning?
Have I used a dictionary to check words that I am not certain of?
Have I checked I have spelt plurals correctly?
Have I checked for words which have double letters?
Have I checked for words which contain silent letters?

Handwriting
Is my handwriting easy to understand?
Have I used capital letters and small letters?
Have I left enough space between words?
Have I left enough space after punctuation?
Have I left enough space between paragraphs?

Appendix 4
Check your mistakes

Write examples of the most frequent mistakes that you make in your writing here.
Write the corrections too. Use this to check any writing you do in future.

Organization	
Layout	
Punctuation	
Grammar	
Capital letters	
Vocabulary	
Spelling	
Handwriting	

Appendix 5
Think about style 1

Friendly and informal		More polite and formal
Who? *People you know well.* Why? *To show friendliness.* Where? *Personal email, letters, etc.*		Who? *Strangers and people you do not know well.* Why? *To show respect.* Where? *Business email, letters, etc.*

Grammar

Friendly and informal		More polite and formal
1 *Present simple* I *want* to ask about … I *wonder* if you can …	→	1 *Present continuous/Past continuous* I *am writing* to enquire about … I *was wondering* if you could …
2 *Direct statements* I *need* you to … (swap this for another one.)	→	2 *Conditional statements* I *would be* grateful …(if you could exchange this.)
3 *Direct requests and questions* Please phone me. How did you lose my order?	→	3 *Indirect requests* Could you please contact me? Could you explain how you lost my order?
4 *Modals* can *and* will *Can* you do this? *Will* you come to my party?	→	4 *Modals* could *and* would *Could* you do this? *Would* you come to my party?
5 *Contractions* I *don't* understand it.	→	5 *No contractions* I *do not* understand it.

Vocabulary

Friendly and informal		More polite and formal
Uses everyday vocabulary ask (about something) ask (for something) buy (something) say sorry (for something) swap (something) tell (someone something) think about (something) email/write to/phone (someone)	→	*Uses specific vocabulary* enquire (about something) request (something) purchase (something) apologize (for something) exchange (something) inform / advise (someone of something) consider (something) contact (someone)

Use a friendly and informal style when you write to people you know well.

Greeting → Saying goodbye

Hi / Hello Pete → Bye for now! / Best wishes,

Thanking someone for something

- *Thanks for …* (a thing, e.g. *your email*).
- *It was lovely to get your …* (thing).

Asking someone to do something

Please can you …?

Telling someone to do something

Send 50 brochures to our Korean office.

Offering to do something

Can I send you a brochure?

Giving news

Guess what? (+ your news)

Checking that people already know something

Do you remember that …? / Did I tell you that?

Saying what you think

I think that …

Checking what other people think

Do you mean …?

Agreeing with someone

You're right to say that …

Saying that you are not certain about something

I partly agree that … / I don't know that …

Disagreeing with someone

You're wrong to say that …

Congratulating someone

Well done!

Closing a letter or email

Hope to hear from you soon. / Write soon.

Use a more polite and formal style when you write to people you do not know well.

- *Dear Mr Johnson, → Yours sincerely,*
- *Dear Sir or Madam, → Yours faithfully,*

- *Thank you for …* (a thing).
- *I am grateful for your …* (thing).

I would be grateful if you could …

Please send 50 brochures to our Korean office.

Would you like me to forward a brochure?

You will be surprised to hear that … (+ your news)

Could you confirm that …?

It is possible that …

Could you confirm you understand that …?

I would agree that …

I would not be sure that …

I am afraid I cannot agree that …

Please accept my congratulations.

I look forward to hearing from you.

Appendix 7
Linking ideas

Linking similar things	Maria is a hard worker *and* she is very experienced. Maria is a hard worker. She is *also* very experienced. Maria is a hard worker. She is very experienced, *too / as well*. *As well as* being a hard worker, Maria is very experienced. (See Unit 5)
Linking positive and negative things	He is intelligent *but* he does not understand computers. He is intelligent. *However*, he does not understand computers. *Although / Even if* he is intelligent, he does not understand computers. (See Unit 9)
Explaining a sequence	*First*, we must develop the product. *Next*, we must train our sales people. *Finally*, we must sell, sell, sell! (See Unit 5) *Before* you cook the microwave meal, put a hole in the lid. *After* the microwave beeps, take out the meal. (See Unit 5) He came to stay. *After that / Afterwards*, he went away again. He came to stay. *Later*, he went away again. (See Unit 11)
Giving examples	*For example*, the MX25 computer sells well. (Abbreviation = e.g.) Our cheaper products are popular, *e.g.* the MX25 computer sells well. (See Unit 10)

Appendix 8
Spelling

Here are some suggestions to help you improve your spelling.

- **Look for patterns. Sometimes pictures can help you remember difficult spellings.**

Look   b e c **a u s** e   Remember   be + c + **aus** + e
              A u s t r a l i a

Think of a spelling that you find difficult. Can you think of a word with a similar spelling pattern? Try to link them together in a picture.

- **Look at these funny sentences from the letters in** *beautiful*.

B ill
e ats
a nything.
U nfortunately,
t hat
i ncludes
F rancine's
u mbrella.
L ovely!

Look at some of your written work and find a word that your teacher always corrects. Make a funny sentence from its letters. Learn the sentence. You won't spell the word incorrectly again!

- **Difficult words like** *advertisement* **may be from a family of words. First learn how to spell the smallest word in the family. It will help you with the others.**

Thing (short form):	*an*	advert
Verb:	*to*	advertise (something)
Person:	*an*	advertiser
Thing (long form):	*an*	advertisement

- **Write a list of words that you often confuse with others or misspell. Every time you write something, remember to check for those words.**

- **For more work on spelling, look at pages 12 (Unit 1, plurals), 21 (Unit 3, /eɪ/, etc.) and 69 (Unit 14, silent consonants and double consonants).**

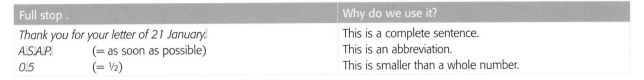

Appendix 9
Punctuation

Full stop .	Why do we use it?
Thank you for your letter of 21 January.	This is a complete sentence.
A.S.A.P. (= as soon as possible)	This is an abbreviation.
0.5 (= ½)	This is smaller than a whole number.

Exclamation mark ! and question mark ?	Why do we use it?
I saw Leonardo Di Caprio yesterday!	This is surprising or important.
Can you repair the drill?	This is a question.

Comma ,	Why do we use it?
We make engines, gears, shafts and other parts for wind turbines.	This is a list.
We use an old Telford pillar drill, TX8745, which has unfortunately broken down.	The information between the commas is extra information.
Before you drive off, check your mirror.	This shows the most important information comes at the end of the sentence.
I need 20,000 brochures printed as soon as possible.	This shows quantities in thousands.

Capital letters	Why do we use it?
Thank you for your letter of 21 January.	This is the beginning of a sentence.
Leonardo Di Caprio, Wednesday, May, French, Japan	This is the name of a person, day, month, language, nationality, place, etc.
How can I help you?	This is a first person pronoun.
A.S.A.P.	This is an abbreviation.

Apostrophe '	Why do we use it?
My sister's office is nearby.	This is the office of my sister.
My sisters' office is nearby.	This is the office of my sisters.
I'm sorry.	This is a contraction. A letter has been missed out.

Audioscript

These recordings are mostly in standard British English. Where a speaker has a different accent, it is noted in brackets.

The recording numbers below are the same as the track numbers on the audio CD.

Unit3

(2) plane   When does your plane leave Berlin?

(3) plane   date   state   name

(4) Spain   My aunt lives in Spain.

(5) stay   How long did you stay in England?

Unit6

(6)

Answerphone: Please leave a message after the tone.

Sara: Hi, Mark, it's Sara. I need your help. I'm in the town centre and I've lost my car keys. I came in to do some shopping and I had to park at the North Car Park. You know they've had problems here, so I checked the car was locked before I left it. I didn't want it to get stolen! Anyway, shopping took longer than I expected. I've been about three hours. I've just got back to the car and I can't find my keys. I think I must have dropped them somewhere. I've been to so many shops that I don't know where to start looking! Can you please come and bring your keys with you? Call me. I'm not going anywhere!

Unit9

(7) (Sinead = Irish, Oleg = Russian, Wen Ling = Chinese)

Sinead: Hello everyone. My name's Sinead and I'd like to welcome you to the Study Centre. Can you all hear me? Oh good. Well, has anyone been here before? No? OK, let me explain what you can do in here. The Study Centre is more than just a place where you can come and sit and do your homework. As you can see, we've got books, DVDs, CDs … er … oh and some computers you can use language learning programs on.

Oleg: Excuse me, can we email from here?

Sinead: The one thing we haven't got here is access to the Internet but you can do that in the … erm … computer room next door. I'll take you there next. Right, in here we have, on the left – above the computers – there are the DVDs and CDs. All the computers have headphones so you can listen and watch them here. With the films and songs – in the folders – are worksheets that you can complete. There are more computers in the Speaking Room, you can use those to practise your pronunciation. Er … by the door here, there's a photocopier. Copies are ten pence each. On the shelves on the right you can see the novels, story books and graded readers and further on there are encyclopedias and factual books for research. If you want any writing practice, that's where you can find the writing books. There are also dictionaries and vocabulary and grammar books on the back shelves.

Wen Ling: Where can we practise for examinations?

Sinead: Oh yes, of course! All exam and business books are kept behind the issues desk. You just have to ask me and I'll get you one. Unfortunately, you can't take those out of the Study Centre though. There aren't many rules here. Apart from the Speaking Room, we do ask you to be quiet and not talk so that people can get on with their work. You can borrow up to six books or one DVD at a time. Oh yes, and er opening times. We're open at lunchtime and after school every day until 8. At the weekend we're open 10 till 2. I think that's all. Has anyone got any other questions?

(8) (Sinead = Irish, Gabriela = Brazilian, Oleg = Russian, Hiroshi = Japanese)

Sinead: This is the computer room. There are … there are many things you can do in here. You can use the Internet, write, collect email, use a lot of different programs. Erm … Your main teacher will give you an individual password to log on. Um, sometimes … sometimes they forget to tell you, so ask your teacher for it! When you do log on you'll find you automatically go to the school's homepage. On it you'll see many useful links … other sites … suggestions for what to do. There are also links to student forums and discussion groups.

Gabriela: What are they?

Sinead: Um … students use these to arrange trips or chat … talk about homework, that sort of thing. There's also links there to the language learning programs. Use the online questionnaire, it's called 'What do I need?' It'll tell you a good program for you to start with. You can practise grammar, vocabulary, prepare for examinations, English for business.

Oleg: Is it possible to print things out?

Sinead: Yes. If you want to print anything out, the printer is in the corner there. We don't charge anything for it but please think about the ink and how many trees are being cut down to make the paper! If you want any help, just ask in the Study Centre. All the computers have a filter on them so you can't log on to any unpleasant websites accidentally.

Hiroshi: And when does it open, please?

Sinead: Yes it's open 8 to 9 every morning before school and it stays open until eight in the evening. On Saturdays and Sundays it opens the same time as the Study Centre. Oh, one last thing, it's very popular, you need to sign up on the booking form on the door. You sign up for half an hour at a time. Is that OK?

Unit 10

🔘 **9** (Extract from the song *Rain, Rain, Beautiful Rain.*)

🔘 **10** (Presenter = Australian, Narrator = Australian)

Presenter: Welcome back. Here at Radio KTN we are continuing the story of Ladysmith Black Mambazo's rise to fame.

Narrator: In 1985 Paul Simon travelled to South Africa in the hope of collaborating with black musicians for his *Graceland* album. Simon asked Ladysmith Black Mambazo to work with him, and they travelled to London to record. The first recording was *Homeless*, composed by Shabalala with English lyrics by Simon. *Graceland* was released in 1986, and although both Joseph Shabalala and Paul Simon were accused of breaking the cultural boycott of South Africa, the album was a success and introduced Ladysmith Black Mambazo into the international arena. This also paved the way for other African acts like Stimela, Mahlathini and the Mahotella Queens to gain popularity with western audiences.

The release of Nelson Mandela from prison was a historic occasion for South Africa. The apartheid system was abolished in 1991 and the group's first release in the post-apartheid era was 1993's *Liph' Iqiniso*. The album's last track, *Isikifil' Inkululeko* (*Freedom Has Arrived*), was a celebration of the end of apartheid.

In 1993, at the request of Nelson Mandela, Ladysmith Black Mambazo accompanied the future President of South Africa to the Nobel Peace Prize ceremony in Oslo, Norway. Mambazo sang again at President Mandela's inauguration in May 1994.

Unit 12

🔘 **11**

a Wind turbines use wind to make electricity.
b 35,000 wind-up radios were given to the people of Aceh after a tsunami in 2005.

🔘 **12**

a Your watch has stopped. You need to wind it up.
b Can you hear the wind in the trees?
c I was cold in the back of the car, so I asked the driver to wind his window up.
d A hurricane is a very fast wind.

Unit 13

🔘 **13** (Luc = French)

Luc: Hello, everyone. Thank you for allowing me to speak to you today. Most of you know me, my name's Luc and I'm fanatical about sports. Today I'm going to talk about the Olympics. Well, everyone knows what the Olympic Games are, or do they? We've all seen them on TV but where do they come from and what's behind them? Are they just an opportunity for overpaid sports men and women to show off? Or are they something much more than that? In this talk I'm going to look at what the Games are and what they stand for. I'll split the talk into four sections: one, a definition of the Olympics; two, their history, three, the core Olympic ideals and four, the Olympic symbols. As I talk, you'll come to see why I believe that the Olympic Games are much more than just a sporting competition. As I've said, I'll break my talk into sections and you're welcome to ask questions at the end of each section.

🔘 **14** (Luc = French)

Luc: Hello, everyone. Thank you for allowing me to speak to you today. Most of you know me, my name's Luc and I'm fanatical about sports. Today I'm going to talk about the Olympics. Well, everyone knows what the Olympic Games are, or do they? We've all seen them on TV but where do they come from and what's behind them? Are they just an opportunity for overpaid sports men and women to show off? Or are they something much more than that? In this talk I'm going to look at what the Games are and what they stand for. I'll split the talk into four sections: one, a definition of the Olympics; two, their history, three, the core Olympic ideals and four, the Olympic symbols. As I talk, you'll come to see why I believe that the Olympic Games are much more than just a sporting competition. As I've said, I'll break my talk into sections and you're welcome to ask questions at the end of each section.

Right, let's start with number one: a definition. The modern Olympic Games are a truly international multi-sport event. At the first modern Olympics only fourteen nations competed but now over two hundred countries send athletes. That's more countries than are officially recognized by the United Nations. The modern Olympic Games are split between the Summer Games and the Winter Games. At the first Games there were just eight sports: athletics, cycling, fencing, gymnastics, weightlifting, shooting, swimming and wrestling, but at the 2012 Summer Games there will be twenty-six. The Winter Games feature sports such as skiing, figure-skating and ice hockey. Since their start, the Summer Games have been held every four years, with just a few interruptions. The Winter Games and the Summer Games are held two years apart. Any questions, so far?

No? Let's move on then to the history of the Games. So how did the multi-sport spectacular start? The first Olympic Games were held in 776 BC in Olympia, Greece and went on to be held every four years for a thousand years. They were designed to stop the constant wars between Greeks who would compete at sports instead. When the ruins of Olympia were discovered in the nineteenth century, people again became interested in the ancient Games. In 1894, Baron Pierre de Coubertin founded the International Olympic Committee and the first modern Olympic Games were held in Athens two years later. The first Winter Games were held in 1924 in Chamonix, France.

OK, the Olympic philosophy. The Olympics are designed to be a festival, a celebration of what humans can do. This festival brings people together, helps them to understand each other and helps build a more peaceful world. The philosophy behind it is summarized by the motto, Citius, Altius, Fortius which means Faster, Higher and Stronger. The main idea is that by excelling in fair sports competition people can make the world a better place. As the Olympic creed says, 'The most important thing is not to win, but to take part'.

The two main symbols of the Olympic Games are the Olympic flame and the flag. Months before a modern Games starts, the Olympic flame is lit from the sun's rays at Olympia, the home of the ancient Olympics. It is then carried by athletes in a relay to the venue for the Games and burns all the time the competitions are taking place. It symbolizes the link between the ancient and modern Games and the handing down of knowledge, life and spirit from generation to generation. The flag is a symbol of international friendship. The five linked rings on it represent the five continents linked together. Each ring is a different colour so that the flag contains colours that are used in all the national flags of the world.

So the flame and the flag neatly sum up what the Olympics is all about. Friendship between countries.

Well, we've looked at a definition of the Games, a brief history and an explanation of their philosophy and symbols. I hope I've been able to persuade you that they are more than just a huge sports competition and that next time you watch them you'll think about the ideals behind the Games. Thank you for listening to me. I'd be happy to answer any questions you may have …

Unit 14

15 (Darren = American)

Darren: Clothes Work 4U.

Maureen: Hello. I'm phoning from Easyclean.

Darren: Yes, what can I do for you?

Maureen: Well, I need to put in an order.

Darren: Fine, I can help you with that. What's your name, please?

Maureen: It's Maureen, Maureen Plumber. That's P-L-U-M-B-E-R.

Darren: And your number there, Maureen?

Maureen: My direct line's 020-7556-7887 and my email's maureen@easyclean.co.uk.

Darren: And what's the company address?

Maureen: It's 15a Tarpit Road, that's T-A-R-P-I-T Road, London W14 7HG.

Darren: Is that the delivery address as well?

Maureen: Yes, they're the same.

Darren: And what was it you wanted?

Maureen: I need ten coveralls with our logo on them.

Darren: Right, just let me look them up in the catalogue … Erm is that the one with the buttons?

Maureen: Yes, that's right.

Darren: What colour and size did you want?

Maureen: I need them in navy blue. Just six large and four medium, please.

Darren: That's fine. That's £9.50 each, a total of £95.00. And when do you want them by?

Maureen: Well, really as soon as possible. I want to show them to the managing director and hopefully put in an order for a lot more.

Darren: OK, normally it takes a couple of weeks, but I'll see what we can do. Will you be emailing the design?

Maureen: No, I'll send it by courier and you should get it this afternoon.

Darren: Excellent! Oh yes, do you want them printed or embroidered? Embroidery costs an extra 50p per garment.

Maureen: Printed is fine.

Darren: Good, we'll look forward to receiving the logo.

16 (Fabio = Portuguese)

Fabio: Hello. It's Fabio Lopez from WGL Technology. I'd like to put in an order for 50 large T-shirts in black. That's 50 T02s. I really need them in long sleeves though, is that possible? We need them for a trade fair at the end of the month so can you get them to me by the 25th of the month? Thanks. You've got the design already and we'd like them printed as usual. We also need 100 black baseball caps. Can you send the invoice and deliver to the normal address? That's WGL Technology, Redgate House, Ipswich, IP24 2HC. If you have any problems, please give me a ring on 01842 763074 or email me at lopezf@wgltech.com. That's L-O-P-E-Z-F at W-G-L-T-E-C-H dot com. Thank you.

17 (Fabio = Portuguese)

Fabio: Hello. It's Fabio at WGL again. I need to change the order I just left on your voicemail. My boss says we've got to go earlier. Can you please get the T-shirts to me by the 20th of this month? And we need 100 T02s, not 50. Thanks.

18 why   write   know   right   black   talk   half   could   design   comb   listen

19 calf   daughter   foreign   knife   quick   thumb   whistle   white   would   wrong

Unit 16

20 (Yuki = Japanese)

Yuki: Hello Martin. I'd like you to email the product development and marketing team involved with Vocscribe. We need to finalize the box design and the marketing campaign for the new version as soon as possible. I want you to set up a meeting for the beginning of next week to look at the box and advertising possibilities. Those need to be the main two items on the agenda. Check with the team if they have anything else they want to discuss at the meeting. Can you fix it all up and get back to me with the time and agenda? Thanks.

Unit 1

Get ready to write

- *Your own answers*
- *Your own answers. Possible answers*:
  your name
  your credit card details
- a (the solar battery charger) is probably the best present

1 Proceed to checkout?
2 Confirm (password)
3 a Shipping address   b Optional   c Billing address
4 a (Airmail is a lot faster than surface mail when you are sending to a different country.)
5 a 7   b 2
6 2 a 3 d 4 b
7 No. (Be careful, it must have a full stop!)
8 There are no spaces in the typed number because spaces would confuse the computer.

Focus on spelling plurals

1 a books   b boxes   c bikes   d toy buses
   e watches   f TVs   g computers
2 diary businessman woman diaries price
3 a universities   b stories   c cities   d memories   e babies

---

9 a Cairo   b Zamalek   c 1511
10 (Suggested answer) The walkie talkies are probably the best present for a six-year-old.
11

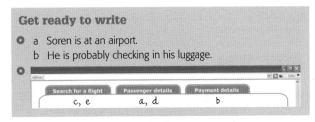

12

Unit 2

Get ready to write

- a Soren is at an airport.
  b He is probably checking in his luggage.
-

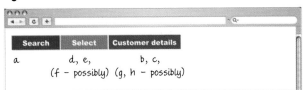

1 a 27 September 2009 in the morning.
  b No. (He is booking a one-way ticket not a return.)
  c No. (Only one adult, no children or infants)
  d All necessary information is marked with an asterisk (*).
  e DD = day of the month
     MM = number of the month
     YYYY = year (e.g. 27/09/2008)
2 a 11.30
  b X8976 (economy fare [He has clicked on the circle ⊙].)
3 1, 5, 6 (These pull-down menus are normally marked with arrows ⬍.)
4 a T
  b F (It may be your home phone number, but it is always the phone number of the place you are travelling to.)
5 b 1   c 2   d 4
6 b ✓   c ✓   d ✓   e ✓   f Probably not.
  g Probably not. This would be dealt with when he picked up the car.
  h Probably not. This would be dealt with when he picked up the car.
7 *Your own answer. Possible answer*:
  The website will probably ask the date he wants to return the car and if he wants any extra things, such as child seats.
8

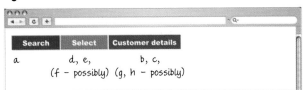

9 *Your own answer. Possible answer:*
Automatic or manual transmission.

10 b 5 c 4 d 1 e 3

11

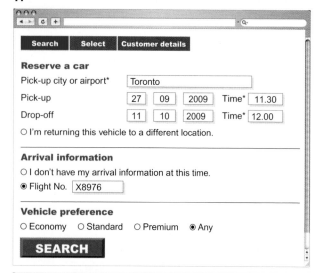

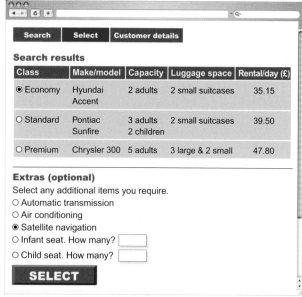

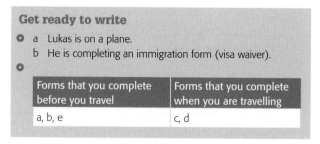

Unit 3

Get ready to write

○ a Lukas is on a plane.
 b He is completing an immigration form (visa waiver).

○

Forms that you complete before you travel	Forms that you complete when you are travelling
a, b, e	c, d

1 b F (We only know that he lives in Germany.)
 c T (We know his address while on holiday in the US.)
 d T (It is a good idea to complete forms using capital letters.)
2 c These sections are for 'government use only'.
3 a 2 b 1
4 *Your own answers*
5 a 104-2 Jeokseon-dong, Jongno-gu, Seoul, 110-052, REPUBLIC OF KOREA
 b 28 Ambrose Street, Fulford, York, YO10 4DR, UK
6 b Seoul c Republic of Korea
7 b not in employment
 c school student
 d mature student
 e employed full-time
 f employed part-time
8 Your *own answer. Possible answer:*
It will probably ask for her date of birth, her contact details in Korea and in the UK and her employment status.
9 a 01904 448871
 b 0082 2 27422354

> **Focus on If..., tick here.** ☐
>
> 1 You will receive your information by phone.
> 2 a
> 3 You should tick the box in b

10

UK Young Person's Railcard Application Form

Title	Mr ☐ Mrs ☐ Miss ☐ Ms ✓ Other ☐	Date of Birth `1 5 0 7 1 9 8 7`
First Name	`H E A H`	
Surname	`K I M`	
Home Address	`1 0 4 - 2 J E O K S O N - D O N G`	
	`J O N G N O - G U`	
Town	`S E O U L , R E P U B L I C O F K O R E A`	
Postcode	`1 1 0 - 0 5 2`	Telephone `0 0 8 2 2 2 7 4 2 2 3 5 4`
Term Address	`2 8 A M B R O S E S T R E E T`	
	`F U L F O R D`	
Town	`Y O R K`	
Postcode	`Y O 1 0 4 D R`	Telephone

If you would like to receive special offers and information by email, please enter your email address clearly and in block capitals here.

Email Address

Occupations   School/FE student ☐   Part-time student ☐   HE/University student ✓
Mature student ☐   Full-time employed ☐   Part-time employed ☐
Not in employment ☐

Renewals   Are you renewing your Young Person's Railcard? Yes ☐ No ✓
If so, what is your existing Railcard Number? ☐
Expiry date of existing Railcard ☐
How many Young Person's Railcards have you held in the past? ☐

Declaration

Before signing this declaration, it is important that you have read, understand and agree to the two sets of conditions shown in this leaflet.
I have read, understood and agree to the two sets of conditions shown in this leaflet. I confirm that the details I have provided are correct and I am aged between 16 and 25 years or a mature student.

Signature *He Ah Kim*   Date `2 6 0 7 2 0 0 7`

The train companies may also wish to contact you directly with details of rail offers and other rail-related services.
If you do NOT wish to be contacted in this way by ATOC Ltd, please tick here. ✓
The information collected may also be passed to third party organisations for them to send you offers of goods and services.
If you do NOT wish ATOC Ltd to make your information available to third parties in this way, please tick here. ✓

Focus on spelling /eɪ/

1 They are all spelt *a* + single consonant + *e*
3 *a* + consonant + *e*
5 *ai*
6 *ay*
7 b train   c pay   d gate

Unit 4

Get ready to write

● a
● *Your own answer*

A

1 b a double en suite room
  c 22nd–24th December
2 a 2 b 1 c 3
3 You are on your own so you will probably ask about a single room.

---

4 *Your own answer. Possible answer:*
I would be grateful if you could let me know if you have a single room available for one night on 25 April.

5 *Your own answer. Possible answer:*
(You may want to find out how far the hotel is from the hot springs. It is strange that the hotel mentions the bus. This might mean it is not very close to the springs.)
Please also send details of the distance from the hotel to the hot springs as I would like to visit them.

6 *Your own answer. Possible answer:*

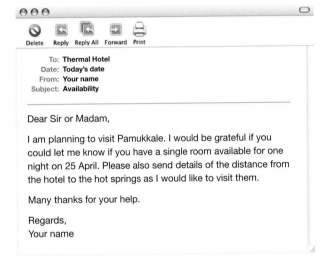

Delete Reply Reply All Forward Print

To: **Thermal Hotel**
Date: **Today's date**
From: **Your name**
Subject: **Availability**

Dear Sir or Madam,

I am planning to visit Pamukkale. I would be grateful if you could let me know if you have a single room available for one night on 25 April. Please also send details of the distance from the hotel to the hot springs as I would like to visit them.

Many thanks for your help.

Regards,
Your name

B

1 b 3 c 9 d 8 e 7 f 1 g 2 h 10 i 5 j 6
2 a 3 b 1 c 2
3 I understand that (+ a statement)
4 *You should underline:* please send your credit card details and home address
5 4489 0122 1221 1248   01/11 (January 2011)
6 *Your own answer. Possible answer:*
I understand that you will charge a deposit of US $3 for a single room.
7 *Your own answer. Possible answer:*

Your address
Today's date

Bulent Demirci
Thermal Hotel
M. Akif Bulvari, 34
Pamukkale 20280
Denizli,
Turkey

Dear Mr Demirci,

Re: Your email

I would like to book a single room for one night on 25 April. My credit card number is 4489 0122 1221 1248 and it expires on 01/11. I understand that I will need to pay a deposit of US $3 per night.

Many thanks for your help.

Yours sincerely,
Your name

Answer key

Focus on *as/since* and *so* (linking reasons and results)

1. b   ✗ (Correct version: *The play starts at 7.30, **so** we advise you to arrive early.*)

   c   ✓

2. *Your own answers. Possible answers*:

   b   Since the play finishes at 11.00, we'll have to eat before we go to the theatre.

   c   Many people visit Pamukkale as the spring water is meant to be good for your health.

   d   The food at the Efes restaurant is brilliant, so I go there every night to eat.

Unit5

Get ready to write

- *Your own answers*
- *Your own answer*

1. 3 (a ready-meal / microwave meal)

2. c (He was probably also in a hurry.)

3. a 2   b 4   c 3   d 1

4. You should underline the following:

   b   Use subject pronouns (e.g. *You* do this) / <u>Don't use subject pronouns</u> (e.g. ~~You~~ do this)

   c   <u>Use the present simple</u> / Use the present continuous

   d   <u>Use sequencers</u> (e.g. First, Next, Finally etc.) / Don't use sequencers (e.g. ~~First, Next, Finally~~, etc.)

Focus on sequences

1. a

3. b   Before you send an email, check your spelling. (Make sure you use a comma.)

   c   Take Bonzo for a walk before you feed him.

   d   After you load the dishwasher, turn it on. (Make sure you use a comma.)

4. *Your own answers. Possible answers*:

   Before you visit the historic sites, read a guide book.

   Change some money into dollars before you leave home.

   After you eat a meal in a restaurant, give the waiter a 10% tip.

---

5. *Your own answers. Possible answers*:

   b   Then, put the washing liquid in the plastic ball.

   c   Next, press (the) number 3.

6. Don't forget / Remember to separate the whites from/and the colours before doing the washing.

7.

> Sorry. Didn't have time to do the washing. Can you do your own?
>
> First, put the white washing in the washing machine.
>
> Then, put the washing liquid in the plastic ball.
>
> Next, press number 3.
>
> Thanks. See you later.
>
> PS Don't forget to separate the whites and colours before doing the washing.

Focus on linking similar things (*and, also, too/as well, as well as*)

2. b 1   c 4   d 2

3. b   You can enjoy Thai food in the restaurant as well as Malaysian food. / As well as Thai food, you can enjoy Malaysian food in the restaurant.

   c   Fish is an important food in Japan. It is also an important food in Norway.

   d   Swiss chocolate is very good. Belgian chocolate is good as well.

   e   Mexican food and Egyptian food can be spicy.

4. *Possible answer*:

> Had to go out. Why don't you get a takeaway? The town's got a good Chinese Noodle Bar. There's also a great kebab shop on the corner of King Street. It sells excellent chips as well as kebabs. If you don't like that, there's also an Indian in King Street.

Unit6

Get ready to write

- The man is sending an SMS / text message.
- *Your own answer*
- b

A

1. b

2. He invites her to go to the cinema with him.

3. b T   c F (They use abbreviations like '2' for 'to/too' and 'c' for 'see', etc.)   d F

4. b ✓   c ✗ (They are only left in if the message would be confusing without them).   d ✗   e ✓

5. b   ~~I'm at the~~ North Car Park.

   c   ~~I've~~ lost my car keys.

   d   ~~Please~~ can you bring ~~your~~ keys?

6. b r   c y   d b   e c   f 2   g 4   h 8

7. b love   c what   d night

---

8 b later
c tomorrow
9 b 4 c 7 d 3 e 2 f 5 g 1
10 b I don't know if I can come.
c She won't be there.
11 *Your own answer. Possible answer:*

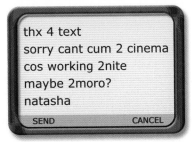

want 2 go out 2nite?
meet @ cinema @ 7.
c u l8r.
artash :-)

SEND   CANCEL

12 *Your own answer. Possible answer:*

thx 4 text
sorry cant cum 2 cinema
cos working 2nite
maybe 2moro?
natasha

SEND   CANCEL

Focus on editing for essential information

2 She has lost her car keys.
4 Hi, Mark, it's <u>Sara</u>. I need your help. I'm in the town centre and <u>I've lost my car keys</u>. I came in to do some shopping and I had to park at the <u>North Car Park</u>. You know they've had problems here, so I checked the car was locked before I left it. I didn't want it to get stolen! Anyway, shopping took longer than I expected. I've been about three hours. I've just got back to the car and I can't find my keys. I think I must have <u>dropped them somewhere</u>. I've been to so many shops that I don't know where to start looking! Can you please <u>come and bring your keys</u> with you? Call me. I'm not going anywhere!

a Sara
b She's lost her car keys.
c North Car Park
d She dropped the keys somewhere.
e She wants him to bring his keys to the car park.

5 a, b, c and e
6 *Possible answer:*

Help! @ North Car Park
lost keys
plz bring yours
luv Sara

B

1 b T c T d T e F
2 a gotta b TTFN
3 b 4 c 1 d 5 e 3

4 *Your own answers. Possible answers:*
b No! How come?
c That's great! ☺
d TTFN
e Shame ☹

Focus on double consonants

~~usefull~~ = useful   ~~begining~~ = beginning   ~~geting~~ = getting
~~writting~~ = writing   ~~imposible~~ = impossible

Extra practice

b ☺ c ☹ d ☹ e ☹ f ☺ g ☺

Unit 7

Get ready to write

○ *Your own answer. Possible answer:*
They are having a party and celebrating something.
○ *Your own answers.*

1 b T c T (The year is not important)
2 a letter.
b to hear from you soon.

Focus on apostrophes 1

1 b won't c she'd d we've e they'll f weren't
2 b It's been a long time since I heard from you.
c I couldn't tell you about the party because it was a surprise.
d They'll celebrate the Chinese New Year at the end of January this year.
e When you've seen the film, you'll understand why I think it's brilliant!
f Here in Turkey, it's the end of Ramazan and we're celebrating Seker bayram at the moment.

3 a Did I tell you that
b Do you remember,
4 Guess what?
5 a any celebrations like this in England?
b any good bands in York?
6 b happy c happy d sad e sad
7 a It's good to hear that
b I'm sorry to hear that
8 1 b 2 a
9 You should underline:
<u>You wrote about Batz.</u>
<u>It's interesting to hear about …</u>
10 *Your own answers. Possible answers:*
a You wrote about Batz. In Turkey, Yeni Turku are really good. They play modern Turkish folk music.
b It's interesting to hear about Fat Thursday. We have a celebration called <u>Seker bayram</u>. On that day we give sweets and presents to children and friends.

11 b Did I tell you / Do you remember
   c Guess what?
12 *Your own answers. Possible answers*:
   b I'm also sorry *that I haven't written recently. I've been very busy, too.*
   c *It's good to hear that* you've got a new job.
   d It's interesting to hear about *Fat Thursday.*
   e We have a similar celebration called *Shrove Tuesday / Pancake Day.*
   f *Do you remember / Did I tell you that* I bought a motorbike last year?
   g *Guess what?* It's broken down and I've bought a new car.
   h *Do you have a / Have you got a* car or a motorbike?
   i I'll write *again soon.*
13 *Your own answer. Possible answer*:

> York
> 13 March
>
> Dear Leszek,
>
> Thanks for your letter. I'm also sorry that I haven't written recently. I've been very busy, too. It's good to hear that you've got a new job. Are you enjoying it more, now?
>
> It's interesting to hear about Fat Thursday. We have a similar celebration called Shrove Tuesday. It's also called Pancake Day because on that day it is traditional to make pancakes and eat them with lemon juice and sugar. They're delicious!
>
> Did I tell you that I bought a motorbike last year? Well, guess what? It's broken down and so I've bought a new car. Do you have a car or a motorbike?
>
> Anyway, I must go now. I'll write again soon.
> Best wishes,
> Peter

Extra practice

Your own answer. Possible answer:

> Cambridge
> 28 July
>
> Dear Suzie,
>
> Thanks for the letter. I'm sorry that I haven't written recently. I've been very busy at work and in the evenings I've been too tired to write! It's good to hear that Dawn won a prize. Has she entered any other competitions recently?
>
> Do you remember you asked about museums? Well, in my town we have a museum called the Cambridge Folk Museum. It's full of everyday things from the last few hundred years. It sounds boring but it isn't! I always like to try to imagine what it was like living when my grandparents were young.
>
> Guess what? Last month, my boss sent me to Canada for a two-week training course and at the weekend we all went skiing. I fell over a lot but it was great! I'll send you the pictures sometime.
>
> I'll write again soon.
>
> Best wishes,
> Graham

Focus on apostrophes 2

1 apostrophe
2 b The garage did my car's annual service last week.
   c Suzanne and Giorgi are my best friends' names.
   d The children's auntie is a middle-aged woman with black hair.
   e My husband's family are very intelligent.
   f The town's main street was very dirty and full of litter.
3 a of b an apostrophe
4 b name of the book c uncle's dog d east of the country

Unit 8

Get ready to write

◉ a *Your own answer*
  b *Your own answer*

A

1 b 1 c 3 d 4 e 6 f 2
2 a 'As you know'… suggests that the writer and reader share some knowledge already.
3 (Different answers are possible)

A journal that anybody on the Internet can read	A journal that your family can read	A journal that only your friends can read
b, c, d, g	b, c, f, g	a, b, c, e, f, g

Focus on blog headings

1 ~~Here is some information about~~ my visit ~~with my sisters~~ to ~~see Mickey Mouse in~~ Disneyland ~~Resort~~, Paris …
2 Petra's calm ride / Petra flies with Peter Pan / Petra and the Pirate
3 *Your own answer. Possible answer* (about a trip to the Cairo Museum):
Fun with the pharaohs

4 *Your own answer*
(If everybody can read it, is there anything you want to leave out so that you don't upset your friends or family?)
5 *Your own answers. Possible answers*:
  a Cairo Museum of Egyptian Antiquities
  b We spent all morning there and looked at a few of the 120,000 ancient Egyptian things that they have there.
  c I loved seeing all the treasures from Tutankhamun's tomb, especially the gold mask.
  d Visit the museum before you visit the temples and tombs in Egypt. It will help you to understand how they looked in the past.

6 *Your own answers. Possible answers:*

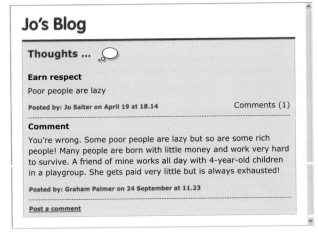

Graham's Blog

My journal 📖

20.02 March 19

Fun with the pharaohs

Visited the Cairo Museum of Egyptian Antiquities today. We spent all morning there and looked at a few of the 120,000 ancient Egyptian things that they have there. There's no way you can see everything in one day! I loved seeing all the treasures from Tutankhamun's tomb especially the gold mask. It's great!

My top tip: visit the museum before you visit the temples and tombs in Egypt. It will help you understand how they looked in the past.   **Comments (0)**

B

1 a (Jo writes about what she thinks, not about what she has done. Although c is a difference, it is not the most important one.)

2 b (Jo's friends and family will probably already know her views. If Jo has many readers, the discussion will be more lively.)

3 c

4 b

5 I partly agree.

6 2 You're wrong.   3 I don't know.   4 I partly agree.
5 You're right.   6 You're absolutely right.

7 *Your own answers*

8 b 3 c 2 d 4

9 *Your own answers. Possible answers:*

Jo's Blog

Thoughts ...

Earn respect

Poor people are lazy

Posted by: Jo Salter on April 19 at 18.14   Comments (1)

Comment

You're wrong. Some poor people are lazy but so are some rich people! Many people are born with little money and work very hard to survive. A friend of mine works all day with 4-year-old children in a playgroup. She gets paid very little but is always exhausted!

Posted by: Graham Palmer on 24 September at 11.23

Post a comment

10 *Your own answers. Possible answers:*

  b You may think that nuclear power is the best way to stop global warming but you're wrong because nuclear pollution lasts for thousands of years.

  c You may think that drugs testing on animals is OK but you're wrong because animals can also feel pain.

  d You may think that politicians always tell lies but you're wrong because some try to fight corruption.

Review 1

A Planning your writing

Choosing what to write

1 d (Unit 8) You might also send an email to all your friends.

2 c (Unit 7)

3 a (Unit 1)

4 c (Unit 4) You might also send an email

5 b (Unit 5)

Knowing the reader

6 b (Unit 6) You do not know if the person will understand symbols and abbreviations.

Choosing information

7 a (Unit 4)

8 a (Unit 8)

9 a (Units 1 and 2)

10 d (Unit 3) (If you tick any of the boxes, the company will contact you.)

B Checking your writing

Checking that the reader has enough information

11 c (Unit 4) (The writer needs to say what kind of room they want.)

12 b (see Unit 5). Your friend's safety is more important than where the bike is and what colour it is!

Checking that the information is well organized

13 d (Unit 7)

14 a (Unit 4)

15 c (Unit 8)

Checking layout

16 d (Unit 7)

17 b (see Unit 4, part B)

Checking punctuation

18 a 1 (Unit 7)   b 2 (Unit 7)

19 d (Unit 7)

Checking grammar

20 b (Unit 5)

21 b (Unit 5) (Correct sentence would be: 'Ready-meals are expensive as well **as** not very healthy.')

22 a (Unit 4)

Checking vocabulary

23 c (Unit 3)

24 c (Unit 6)

25 b (Unit 8)

Checking spelling

26 b (Unit 1) (correct spelling = matches)

27 c (Unit 3)

Unit 9

Get ready to write

○ *Your own answers. Possible answers*:
What can I do in the study centre?
When can I use it?
Do I have to pay to use the study centre?

○ Order she mentions things:
Opening times? 6
Email? 1
What can I borrow? 5
Business English? 4
Pronunciation? 2
Photocopies? 3

A

1 (The mistake is circled below – the study centre is open until 2.00 pm at the weekends.)

Study Centre
Opening times?
Monday–Friday: lunchtime + after school – 8.00
Weekends: 10.00 – 12.00

2 He has added an extra note ('N.B. Find out about computer room opening times')
3 a 3 b 2 d 4
4 b 3 c 1 d 5 e 4
5 *Your own answer. Possible answer*:

a When open?
b What can I do?
c Booking?
d Print out?

6 *Your own answer.*
7 *Your own answer. Possible answer*:

Computer Room
When open?
Monday–Friday: 8.00 – 9.00 (before school)
                    + after school – 8.00
Weekends: same as study centre
What can I do? – Internet/email
– practise grammar, vocabulary, examinations,
English for business
Booking? Sign up on door
Print out? Yes (be careful!)
NB Get password from teacher.

Focus on linking positive and negative comments (*but, however, even if, although*)

1 b This mobile phone sends video. However, it's expensive.
c Although your friend is very handsome, he's not very intelligent. / Your friend is very handsome, although he's not very intelligent.
2 The camera is well-made, even if it is ugly. It can take pictures in the day. However, it doesn't have a flash.

B

1 Yes, he was happy with it. (He gives the teaching and most of the facilities a rating of 1–3. The only thing he found poor was the living accommodation [rating 5])
2 a 2 b 1 c 3
3 *Your own answer. Possible answer*:
A computer
4 *Your own answer.*
5 b Companies normally want to know first what you expected from the product.
6 *Your own answers. Possible answers*:

+	–
It does things fast.	It was expensive.
It's good for surfing the Internet.	Some of my old programs won't work on it.

7 *Your own answers. Possible answers*:

Customer Satisfaction Survey

Name Your name

Product HL567 computer

1 Why did you choose this product? How important were these things to you when you made your choice? Rank them. (1= most important, 3 = least important)

The manufacturer's reputation [2]
The product's special features [1]
The price [3]

2 How did you first hear about this product? Tick ✓ one.

Advertisement ☐
Friend's recommendation ☐
Display in a shop ☑
Internet ☐
Other ☐ (Please say what: _____)

3 How much do you agree with these statements? Tick ✓ one box.
(1= completely agree, 5 = completely disagree)

	1	2	3	4	5
I am satisfied with the product.	☐	☑	☐	☐	☐
The product is useful.	☐	☑	☐	☐	☐
The product is well designed.	☑	☐	☐	☐	☐

4 Would you recommend this product to a friend? Why or why not?

I love the HL567! It does things really fast and looks great. Even if it was expensive, it's good for surfing the Internet. However, some of my old programs won't work on it. Can you fix them?

Unit 10

Get ready to write

○ b

○ *Your own answers. Possible answers*:
Are they famous?
Have they recorded many songs?
When did they start singing together?

○ *Your own answers. Possible answers*:
Yes, they are famous.
They have recorded songs with Paul Simon and their own album, Amabutho. But we don't know how many songs they have recorded.
The group formed in 1964.

1 b 1 c 1 d 1 e 2 (They formed in 196**4** and they met **Paul Simon** and recorded Graceland.)

2 1 (This set of notes is easiest to read and contains most information.)

3 b T c T d F e T (The reporter who wrote Notes 1 already knows Paul Simon and has added an explanation of who he is.) f T g T h F (You organize your notes by choosing the most important information for you. This may be different to the organization of the book or website.)

4 a (A band website is designed to promote the band and will probably only have good things about them on it!)

5 a 1 b 2

6 a 2 b 1

7 a

8 a

9 ~~In 1985 Paul Simon travelled to South Africa in the hope of collaborating with black musicians for his~~ *~~Graceland~~* ~~album. Simon asked Ladysmith Black Mambazo to work with him, and they travelled to London to record.~~ The first recording was *Homeless*, composed by Shabalala with English lyrics by Simon. *Graceland* was released in 1986, and although both Joseph Shabalala and Paul Simon were accused of breaking the cultural boycott of South Africa, the album was a success and introduced Ladysmith Black Mambazo into the international arena. This also paved the way for other African acts like Stimela, Mahlathini and the Mahotella Queens to gain popularity with western audiences.

10 a

11 <u>post-apartheid</u>

12 Notes need to be short! They would probably only mention the end of apartheid once. They could use *The end of apartheid* as a heading to group the other facts under.

13 c (The notes in a & b are confusing: LBM didn't win the Nobel prize with Mandela!)

Focus on symbols and abbreviations

Comparing things or ideas
1 b 3 c 1 d 2 e 6 f 5

Linking things and ideas
2 a 3 b 2 c 1

Giving examples and explaining
3 b 3 c 4 d 1
4 b ↗ c N.B. d ≠ e > f → *or* ∴

---

14 *Your own answer. Possible answer*:

1986: Shabalala & Simon break cultural boycott of SA. LBM introduced African acts to the world. African acts, e.g. Stimela, Mahlathini, Mahotella Queens, etc.

1991: Apartheid abolished.

1993: LMB album Liph' Iqiniso celebrates end of apartheid.

1993: Nelson Mandela – Nobel Prize. Takes LBM.

1994: LBM at President Mandela's inauguration.

Unit 11

Get ready to write

○ b

○ a

○ *Your own answers. Possible answers*:
Farm labourer: *What's it like in different countries?*
Soldier: *What's it like feeling safe?*

2 a

3 a

4 b

5 a

6 a

7 a 3 b 1 c 2

8 a Who?
b Where?
c What happened?

9 a (Len chooses his words to show his disagreement.)

10 b (No one likes being described in a negative way. Len knew that his father would not read the story: he was no longer alive when it was written.)

11 *Your own answers. Possible answers*:
Mother got up and kissed him and Father sat there and said, 'How are you?'

12 b wore c sat d had e stood f hid g saw

13 a (The poppy as a symbol of the coat would make the British reader think of soldiers who have died.)

14 *Your own answers. Possible answers*:
a I was kicked by a horse.
b I was happy to be with my friend's horse.
c Older boys were throwing stones at the horse.

d I was shocked, angry and in pain. I was also worried that my parents would stop me going riding.

e It was important because I tried to hide it from my parents.

Focus on symbolism

1 *Your own answers. Possible answers*:
   b 2 c 1 d 4 e 3
2 *Your own answers. Possible answers*:
   b distance / nature hiding the soldier forever
   c sadness/loneliness

---

15 *Your own answers. Possible answers*:

Who?	A ten-year-old country girl ('me' in the story). A gang of horrible, older boys from the city. A nervous horse.
Where?	On a quiet country road.
What happened?	The boys hid. I wasn't riding. I was leading the horse. The boys threw stones and the horse panicked, turned and kicked me very hard. I fell to the ground and the boys ran off.

16 *Your own answers. Possible answers*:

a My parents didn't know that I was taking my friend's horse for a walk.

b I really wanted to learn to ride but my parents didn't like me being around horses.

Focus on time sequencers

1 b ✗ c ✓ d ✓
2 *Your own answers. Possible answers*:
   The Chinese invented fireworks. Afterwards, / Later, / Many years later, / After many years, the Germans made rockets that could reach space.

17/18/19 *Your own answer. Possible answer*:
(The writer has added the symbols of the river and the bridge.)
When I was ten, we lived on the edge of the city and I was very jealous of my friend. She had her own horse called Jess and kept her in a field on the other side of the river. My parents are city people. 'You must never go near that horse,' said Dad. 'It's dangerous!' I often stood near the bridge on our side of the river watching as my friend rode her horse on the other side. Jess was so gentle.

One week my friend was ill and couldn't exercise her horse. My heart jumped as I crossed the bridge with the big river racing beneath me. Jess was nervous but she let me tie the rope on and lead her out of the field. We were halfway across the bridge when it happened. A small stone fell with a crack! Then another came and another! It was city boys trying to scare me but I didn't care: I had Jess! Then a stone hit her, she panicked, turned and kicked. I saw the kick and then felt it as pain raced up my leg and blood started trickling down. I hated those boys! What would I tell my parents?

Extra practice

Your own answer. Possible answer:
(c A time when something happened that you were not prepared for).
I was white and shaking. I was going to die. Here I was on a rock, two hundred and seventeen metres above the crashing waves of the Atlantic Ocean and thirteen kilometres from the nearest land. I didn't care that I'd just got married and this was my honeymoon. I didn't care that my beautiful, adventurous wife was standing calmly next to me. I didn't care that I was surrounded by wonderful natural beauty. All that I cared about was that I knew I was going to fall into the ocean! No-one was there to save me: the tiny fishing boat that had brought us to Skellig Michael was now halfway back to the mainland and wouldn't return for hours. I was twenty-six years old and I didn't know I was terrified of heights! I didn't know!

Walking to the very top of this underwater mountain was fine: you could see the ground in front of you. Then you turned round and all you could see was the ocean!

'It's okay. Just don't look down!' said my wife but down was the only way I could look. Down was where we had to go!

Unit 12

Get ready to write

○ *Your own answer.*

○ b (At the time of publication, Europe used most wind energy but Asia was catching up fast.)

○ *The answers are given at the end of Exercise 1, below.*

1 b blade c tower d shaft e generator f cable
2 b 2 c 1
3 b F c T d F (Experts in wind-power would not need an explanation of what wind turbines are.) e T
4

Business/scientific descriptions	Personal descriptions
a, d, e	b, c, f

Focus on the passive form

1 b 2 c 2
2 b use c store d be recharged e wind up

---

5 a, c, d
6

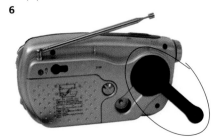

---

7 a

8 *Your own answers. Possible answers*:
How do they work?
Do they have batteries?

9 *Your own answers. Possible answers*:
Wind-up radios work by hand-power.
They have batteries that can be recharged.

Learning tip

2 b 1 c 2 d 1

Focus on linking ideas and thoughts

a 4 b 1 c 3 d 2

10 *Your own answer. Possible answer*:
Wind-up radios use human power to generate electricity. They were developed to help people in places where there is no electricity grid. The radio is wound up with a handle which is connected to a small generator. Turning the handle turns the generator and produces electricity. This electricity is stored in a battery. Winding for 30 seconds generates enough electricity for you to listen to music or news for 30 minutes. Some wind-up radios can also be torches.

Extra practice

Your own answer

Unit 13

Get ready to write

○ It represents the Olympic Games.

○ *Your own answers. Possible answers*:
It's a sports event.
It happens every four years.
It's held in different countries.

○ *Your own answers. Possible answers*:
When did the Olympic Games start?
Why did the Olympic Games start?
Which country has won the most medals at the Olympic Games?

○ *Your own answer*

A

1 b T c F (They include the essential point only – not full sentences.) d T e F f T g T h T

2 a

3 The best place to divide the section would be between the sentences: 'It symbolizes the link between the ancient and modern games and the handing down of knowledge, life and spirit from generation to generation' and 'The flag is a symbol of international friendship'.

4 *Your own answer. Possible answer*:
2 symbols: flame + flag

5 *Your own answer. Possible answer*:
Flame

6

> - lit from <u>sun's rays</u> at <u>Olympia</u> → (relay) → modern venue
> - burns during games
> - links <u>ancient</u> → <u>modern Games</u> OR <u>generation</u> → <u>generation</u>
> - symbolizes knowledge, <u>life</u> and <u>spirit</u>

7 *Your own answer. Possible answer*:
Flag

8

> - symbolizes <u>international friendship</u>
> - 5 rings = <u>five continents</u>
> - 5 colours - <u>colours from every country's flag</u>

9 *Your own answer. Possible answer*:
Flame + flag = Olympics (friendship between countries)

10 *Your own answers. Possible answers*:

SYMBOLS (Slide 5)
2 symbols: flame and flag
Flame
- lit from sun's rays at Olympia → (relay) → modern venue
- burns during games
- links ancient → modern games
- symbolizes knowledge, life and spirit
Flag
- symbolizes international friendship
- 5 rings = five continents
- 5 colours - colours from every country's flag

B

1 a 4 b 2 c 3 d 1

2 The section about symbols does not have a slide.

3 You should tick the following boxes:
b c e

4 b

Focus on planning a presentation

Your own answers.

5 No, you would probably only include the highlighted (most important) information on the slide.

6 Yes

7 Symbols

8 *Your own answer. Possible answer:*

Presentation1.ppt

Symbols

Flame
- links ancient and modern games
- symbolizes knowledge, life and spirit

Flag
- symbolizes international friendship
5 rings = five continents
5 colours = colours from every country's flag

Slide 1 of 1

Unit 14

Get ready to write

- c
- b 2 c 1 d 3

1 There are two mistakes:

1 He has spelt the contact's second name incorrectly. It should be *Plumber* (not *Plumer*).

2 He has written the wrong quantity of large and medium coveralls:

Code	Item	Colour	Size	Qty	Unit Price	Total
C02	Button-up coveralls	Navy	L	~~4~~ 6	9.50	38.00
"	"	"	M	~~6~~ 4	"	57.00

2 b 2 c 4 d 1

3 b T c F d T e T

4 Urgent

6 b ~~We have some larger people working for us. We~~ need T-shirts in XXL.

c ~~Can you do~~ long sleeve ~~not short sleeve~~ T-shirts, ~~please?~~

d ~~Please treat these coveralls with chemicals to~~ make ~~them~~ flameproof. ~~They are~~ (for fire safety officers.)

e ~~We also~~ need bags ~~in the~~ (same design).

7 *Your own answers. Possible answers:*

b Need in XXL

c Long sleeves, pls!

d Make flame-proof (for fire safety officers)

e Need bags (same design)

8 *Your own answers. Possible answers:*

Order form — Clothes Work 4U

Job No.: 0045684

Company: WGL Technology

Contact: Fabio Lopez

Tel.: 01842 763074

Email: lopezf@wgltech.com

Long sleeve T-shirts pls! (good customer)

Invoice address: WGL Technology, Redgate House, Ipswich, IP24 2HC

Delivery address: "

Design delivered: yes | Print / ~~Embroider~~

Date required by: 25th of this month

Code	Item	Colour	Size	Qty	Unit Price	Total
T02	T-shirt	Black	L	50	4.50	225.00
H01	Cap	Black	-	100	1.50	150.00

Extra practice

1 Date required: 20th
T02 Qty: 100

2 *Your own answer. Possible answer:*
NB: WGL phoned again (need T-shirts early)
Do by 20th

Focus on silent consonants and double consonants

1

wh	*wr*	*kn*	*ght*	*ck or ck*
why	write	know	right	black
whistle	wrong	knife	daughter	quick
white				

lk / lf / ld	*gn*	*mb*	*st*
talk	design	comb	listen
half	foreign	thumb	whistle
could			
calf			
would			

3 b When you get to the office, **k**nock on the door and walk straight in.

c The plane is about to land, please fas**t**en your seat belt.

d W**h**ich type of shirt do you want to order?

e The plum**b**er couldn't repair the toilet.

f I'm afraid you sent the **w**rong thing.

4 di**ff**icult busine**ss** rea**ll**y helpfu**l** impo**ss**ible

Unit 15

Get ready to write

- She is making some furniture.
- b
- You should underline:
  a Unfortunately, it has broken
  b … if it is possible for you to make a part
- They will probably reply to her with information that answers her enquiry.

1 Yes

2 a 2 c 3 d 4

3 forward to hearing from you

4 b I have pleasure in attaching a brochure.
   c … should not pose a problem
   d I would be happy to discuss …
   e Please feel free to contact me (direct)

Focus on punctuation and capital letters

1 The correct version is:

> Your school, the A1 Business School, was recommended by a friend. I would be grateful if you could help me. My company is interested in developing some of its workers' English language skills.

2 b The cost is £3.69 per item.
  c Please send a catalogue.
  d My brother, Steve, is a mechanic.
  e N.B. Send 500 brochures today!
  f We sent 35,000 brochures yesterday.
  g If you want to, please come to the meeting.
  h I'm afraid I can't help you with your enquiry.
  i My company's head office is in Oslo.
  j After you have spoken to him, please let me know.

5 b a quote / a brochure c a quote / a brochure
   d a quote / a brochure e your requirements / your enquiry / your letter

6 d (Answers a, b, c and e = many. A few = not many)

7 *Your own answers. Possible answers*:
   b As you will see, we fix all types of computers.
   c As you will see, we supply a variety of cleaning services.
   d As you will see, we sell all kinds of stationery.

8 *Your own answers. Possible answers*:
   a custom-made language courses
   b leaflet / brochure
   c we run a variety of courses
   d £1,000 for each employee; 30

9 *Your own answers. Possible answers:*

File Edit View Insert Format Tools Message Help

From: A1 Business School
Date: 7 May
To: alexi@romanovnet.ru
Subject: English course

Thank you for your enquiry about our language courses. I have pleasure in attaching a document about custom-made courses.

As you will see, we run a variety of courses, so designing a course for you should not pose a problem. The cost would be £1,000 per employee for a course of 30 hours a week. I would be happy to discuss your specific requirements. Please feel free to contact me direct.

I look forward to hearing from you.

Focus on common spelling mistakes

1 2 ✗ 3 ✗ 4 ✗ 5 ✓ 6 ✗ 7 ✗ 8 ✗ 9 ✓ 10 ✗
  11 ✗ 12 ✗ 13 ✓ 14 ✗ 15 ✓ 16 ✗ 17 ✗
  18 ✗ 19 ✗ 20 ✗

2 2 advertisement 3 interested 4 different 6 their
  7 Unfortunately 8 because 10 holidays 11 believe
  12 available 14 little 16 comfortable 17 Please
  18 write 19 grateful 20 could

3 *Your own answers.*

Unit 16

Get ready to write

- b
- *Your own answers*
- a

A

1 b Yuki has asked me to contact you …
   c She would like to invite you all to meet here …
   d The main focus of discussion will be how to promote the product.
   e Please advise me …
   f Regards,

2 b @ c cc d P.A. e M.D.

3 a contact you b advise c attend

4

What do you write …	… to a colleague that you don't know well?	… to a colleague you do know well?
… to greet someone?	**a** Dear colleague,	**b** Dear Martin,
… to explain the reason for the email?	**c** I'm emailing you to invite you …	**d** Just to let you know …
… to make an invitation?	**e** Would you like to attend …?	**f** Would you like to come to …?
… to ask for a response?	**f** I would be grateful if you could reply …	**h** I need an answer …
… to close the email?	**i** Best regards,	**j** Best wishes,

5 A Communication Training Session.

6 *Your own answer. Possible answer*:
The email is too informal. Also, it doesn't give detailed information.

7 a You could underline the following: <u>Making your voice heard in a noisy world</u> (the title), <u>Tuesday, 12 May,</u> (the date) <u>1600–1700</u> (the time), <u>New Meeting Room</u> (the place), <u>Sheila Peacock</u> (the trainer's name)

b *Nice weather today*.

c No. (*Yuki thinks…* should come before *We're having a training session*.)

d No. (The email will go to people who the writer does not know. It is too friendly and informal [i.e. it cuts out words, uses contractions and a direct question. See *Appendix 5 Think about style 1*, page 89].)

e No. (They are not told who to reply to or how to reply [e.g. by phone/email].)

8 *Your own answer. Possible answer*:

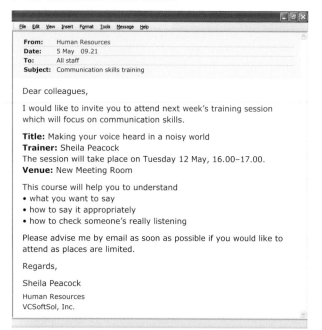

Extra practice

Your own answer. Possible answer:

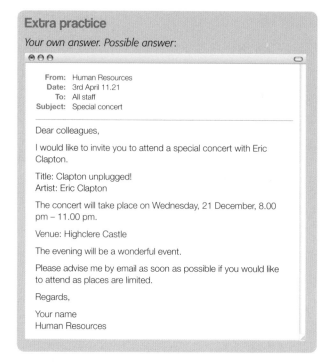

B

1 a The Vocscribe meeting
b On Monday morning, from 9.30 until 11.00
c The Peabody Building

2 <u>prompt</u>

3 [I am happy] to confirm …

4 You should underline:
<u>It will be held in the New Meeting Room and will finish by 11.00.</u>

5 I will look forward to seeing you on Monday.

6 a Communication Training Session / Making your voice heard in a noisy world
b Tuesday 12 May, 1600–1700
c New Meeting Room

7 *Your own answer. Possible answer*:
Refreshments (cakes and hot drinks) will be provided.

8 *Your own answer. Possible answer*:

I am happy to confirm that you have a place at the Communication Training Session 'Making your voice heard in a noisy world' on Tuesday 12 May from 1600–1700.
The session will take place in the New Meeting Room of the Peabody Building. Refreshments (cakes and hot drinks) will be provided.

Extra practice

Your own answers. Possible answers:
I am happy to confirm that you have a place at the 'Clapton unplugged!' event on Wednesday, 21 December from 8.00 pm – 11.00 pm.
The concert will take place at Highclere Castle.

Review 2

A Planning your writing
Choosing what to write

1 d (Unit 12)
2 b (Unit 13)
3 c (Unit 15)
4 a (Unit 9)

Knowing the reader

5 a (Unit 16 and *Think about style 1* page 89)
6 b (Unit 16 and *Think about style 1* page 89)

Choosing information

7 d (Unit 13)
8 b (Unit 14)
9 b (Unit 10)

B Check
Checking that the reader has enough information

10 c (Unit 14). (The reader needs to know the code for the trousers.)
11 d (Unit 10). (All the other information is useful.)
12 a (Unit 15)
13 a (Unit 13) It gives the essential information.

Checking style

14 b (Unit 16)
15 *Your own answer. Possible answers*:
I would be grateful if you could send me a brochure. (Units 15 and 16)

Checking punctuation

16 c (*Price* does not need a capital letter (Unit 15 and *Punctuation* page 93) Note: [answer b] it is not always necessary to use full stops to punctuate NB.
17 N.B. (or NB or NB:) They want to order 15 shirts, 6 pairs of trousers and 5 pairs of gloves. (Unit 15 and *Punctuation* page 93)
18 (Unit 14)

Contact	Company	Job	Email
Suzanne Parker	Clothes work 4U	Managing director	parkerS@clotheswork4U.co.uk
Darren Hall	"	Sales Executive	enquiries@clotheswork4U.co.uk

Checking grammar

19 b (Unit 12) You are interested in what happens, not who does it.
20 b (Unit 9)
21 a (Unit 11)
22 a (Unit 14)

Checking vocabulary

23 b (Unit 15) [You enclose something in a letter and attach something to an email.]

Checking spelling

24 b (Unit 14) now = know.
25 b (Unit 14) correct spelling: useful